For
SHIRLEY
&
GEORGE !

Peter Ford
8/19/06

Ground Clutter— the Book

by

Ralph Hood, CSP

Dedication

This book is dedicated to readers of *AIRPORT BUSINESS*. Thanks to their input by e-mail, telephone—and yes, cards and letters—writing my regular column, Ground Clutter, therein has been more fun than chore.

Acknowledgements

There are two people without whom this book would not exist—Wife Gail and editor John Infanger. This is all their fault!

Wife Gail has more hours invested in this book than I do. All I had to do was write the columns and updates. Gail edited, compiled, corrected, and amended. She also—once I started listening to her—talked me out of several columns that could have caused problems.

AIRPORT BUSINESS editor John Infanger has personally edited each and every column I have written for my column Ground Clutter since 1986. We have fought, argued, and disagreed many times—in fact, that's one of the things I like about John. You can argue heatedly with him with no hard feelings on either side. Besides, I must say about John, quoting from Rudyard Kipling's great poem "Gunga Din," "You're a better man than I am, Gunga Din." A true wordsmith, John made each column better, and, more importantly, he rejected outright many a weak column.

Table of Contents

Foreword

In '86 I came to know
the man some call 'the Hood,'
flamboyant and full of zest
he spoke as few others could.
Our columnist from day one
with *FBO*, then *AIRPORT BUSINESS,*
the loyalty that readers showed
was nothing short of a sickness.
He makes you laugh, makes you think
endears you along the way,
a free-market thinker in Southern clothes
who thinks guvmint should stay away.
Then there's the airlines he so needs
as he speaks across the nation,
he says the way that they've evolved
is sheer abomination.
A man of logic and common sense
who disarms you with his drawl,
he earned his wings at Moontown and the like
talking aviation with one and all.
Enjoy this book? How could you not?
It's 20 years of Ralph's insight,
the knowing smile it brings one's lips
will surely last all through the night.

—J. F. Infanger

Preface

Back in 1986, Mike Murrell and Jon Pellegrin of Johnson Hill Press informed me that the company was planning to publish a magazine called *FBO*. They wondered if I would be interested in writing for it. I was, particularly when I found out they were going to pay me! I had never been paid to write before. Also, I had just left my job selling and insuring airplanes to become a full-time professional speaker and was scared to death the Hood family was going to starve. I was delighted to have at least one regular paycheck.

The first issue of *FBO* came out at the end of that year, and, sure enough, my column, Ground Clutter, was printed therein. I was really quite amazed. And they really did pay me!

Writing that column turned out to be the longest-running job I have ever had. The magazine changed its name to *AIRPORT BUSINESS* in 1993, to reflect more accurately the changing nature of the industry and the magazine, but my column—still called Ground Clutter—still runs in every issue. Through a series of business deals I never fully understood, the company was sold and evolved into Cygnus Business Media, Inc. along the way. Today, editor John F. Infanger and I are the only people currently working on the magazine who were there for that first issue in 1986. It's hard for me to believe that John, and so many other fine folks at Cygnus, have put up with me for all of those years, but he has, and has become a good friend, too.

This book includes some of my favorite columns from almost 20 years of Ground Clutter. Following each column is an "update" written at the end of 2005. The updates brag a little when time proved the original column right—and grovel a bit when the reverse is true.

A lot has changed in aviation since 1986. It has been a privilege to watch, and a bigger privilege to report on it. I appreciate both privileges and appreciate the readers of Ground Clutter most of all.

Ralph Hood

1986 & 1987

1986: The first issue of the new magazine, FBO, came out at the end of 1986. I was 45 years old, which felt old then, but seems young now. I had just celebrated my first full year without smoking and my first full year as a self-employed professional speaker. "Platoon" won the Oscar for best picture. I didn't see it. All adults of 1986 remember exactly where we were when we learned that we had lost Space Shuttle Challenger.

1987: "The Last Emperor" won the Oscar for best picture. I actually saw it. The stock market crash of 1987, including Black Monday, was the steepest in history. One of my columns in FBO was nominated for an award but did not get it. As far as I know, the column was never, ever, nominated thereafter!

Hang onto your charter certificates! (Nov/Dec 1986)

When I was a wee tad in Georgia, the Good Ol' boys wore baseball caps—the closest thing we had to bumper stickers— advising, "Hang onto your confederate money boys, the South's gonna rise again!"

Well, confederate money is still worth about as much as an Aircoupe dealership, and that's not going to change anytime soon. But hang onto your charter certificates and fuel trucks boys, 'cause our share of business travel just *has* to grow.

I'm basing that on one fact: The airline system is falling apart. It is no longer dependable.

I know, you rode the airlines once in August and everything worked fine. Folks, by the time I get home today—if I get home today—I will have airlined across this continent six times in one month. And I say the system ain't working.

I went to Alabama, California, Alabama, Washington (state), Missouri, Alabama, Illinois, Georgia, California, Minnesota and, hopefully, back to Alabama. I can remember one day that the system delivered as promised—one day!

I tried every trick. I left as early as possible on each leg to give myself ample emergency time. I got advance boarding passes. I showed up early for each flight. If the system will work at all, it should have worked for me.

One day I got to bed at 5 in the morning and got up an hour and a half later to teach an all-day class in aviation management. That's rough on a 45-year-old fat man, and you can bet your Jepp case I didn't plan to do it that way. That's not the way I planned it, and that's not what my ticket said either, but, by golly, that's the way the airlines delivered the product.

Another day, during a moment of temporary insanity (caused, no doubt, by the stress of dealing with airlines), I checked my baggage. Now my mother raised me better than that, and I know better.

I was appropriately punished for my sins.

While I reached my destination (two hours late) that day, my baggage didn't. It was delivered to the hotel late that night. By then, the clothes had permanent wrinkles and I had an equally permanent tic in my right eyelid.

As I write this, I'm sitting in an airliner in Minneapolis. According to my ticket, this airplane was supposed to leave one hour and two minutes ago but it didn't, and it still hasn't.

Will this flight leave in time to get me to Memphis in time to catch a flight to Alabama in time to make a speech tonight? I don't know. I do know that a lot of people expect me to be there. I do know that the local media said I will be there. But I don't know if I will be there, and that is the stuff of which ulcers, hypertension, and angina are made.

Now folks, I readily admit that I don't know exactly why the system is failing. But I'll tell you who does know—the airline employees.

Practically every employee on every airline will agree that the whole system is going to hell with the gear and flaps down and the speed brakes fully extended. And, they will tell you exactly what caused it: deregulation.

From the oldest captain to the newest ticket agent, with the flight attendants thrown in, they will all tell you that deregulation is the culprit.

As near as I can tell, deregulation caused acne, the San Andreas Fault, the national debt, and is probably why Johnny can't read.

Has your spouse been a little grouchy lately? Did your stock go down while the market went up? Check it out, good buddy, it probably all started just about the time they deregulated the airlines.

Hogwash!

As a currently popular country and western song puts it, that rock won't roll.

Deregulation didn't cause the problems. Some of them were caused by an addiction to regulation. When a drug addict quits cold turkey, he suffers withdrawal pains. Only a fool would say this withdrawal pain proves that not quitting is good.

The airlines are suffering withdrawal symptoms caused by cold-turkey deregulation.

Back to my original observation: The airlines no longer provide a dependable, comfortable, and timely means of transportation. This has to be good for general aviation business travel.

The business traveler will put up with just so much hassle before he/she looks for an alternative. We're going to get our chance. Let's be ready.

Deliver as promised. Treat people like you appreciate their business. Smile. Tote their bags. Provide the quick turn for your transients and deliver your charter customers on time. Provide a better alternative.

We've got a better mousetrap and it appears the competition has abdicated the throne. Surely goodness and business travelers will come to us and we will dwell in the house of net profit in the years ahead!

Ralph's Update:

I was both right and wrong on this one—right, because airline travel has indeed become less enjoyable and charter more pleasant and more important. But I was wrong in that I missed entirely the biggest change in the use of general aviation for business transportation. That change was fractional ownership. Today, many think the very light jet will be the biggest such change in the future, but the jury is still out on that.

Don't look now, but somebody wants to outsource with you (Jan/Feb 1987)

Perhaps a little background is in order:

When I was in college, they taught us about "the economies of scale." As near as I can recall, according to the economies of scale, the bigger the business, the more economically efficient is the business.

For example, if you made a million widgets a year, your overhead was bound to be lower per widget than if you were producing just 100,000 widgets per year.

Thus, the big guy could sell widgets cheaper than the little guy and eventually force said little guy to his knees. This was supposedly one of the inherent problems of the free market system.

Recently I learned a new buzzword: outsourcing. This was a big factor when one of the major airlines renegotiated the labor contract. Management wanted to outsource; the union didn't want them to do such a thing.

Outsourcing is nothing more nor less than subcontracting, getting something from an outside source.

Now, boys and girls, can you guess whom the great big airline wants to outsource *with*? Why, with smaller companies—companies such as yours.

Hold on now—this is getting confusing. If the economies of scale apply, how come this huge airliner wants to outsource with the little FBO?

I'll tell you why: because sometimes the economies of scale work backward.

For years, the big boys agreed to most everything labor wanted and they passed the cost on to the customer. It worked in Detroit because they pretty much had the only ballpark. It worked with the airlines because of regulation.

Well, imports hit Detroit and deregulation "whupped the airline industry up 'side the head." The consumer had a choice, and when that happens, folks, the consumer decides what he/she is willing to pay. And the consumer ain't even near willing to support the wages and benefits those big boys agreed to when they were protected by regulation.

The big boys are locked into long-term labor contracts negotiated during a protected era that no longer exists. They can't get out. They can, however, outsource with you.

You can do most anything they need done at your airport cheaper than they can do it. And you can make a good profit doing it.

During a workshop I presented at the 1986 National Air Transportation Association convention, I asked the question, "How many of you have contracts with the airlines?" Hands went up all over the room. Then I asked, "How many of you had those contracts ten years ago?" Hands came down. The difference was dramatic.

Fifteen years ago, there was general aviation and there were the airlines, and never the twain did meet (whatever that means). The situation has changed.

I recently visited Martin Aviation at John Wayne Airport in Irvine, CA. They were providing ticket counter and ramp space for an airline! The ticket counter was right there in the FBO lobby, and passengers were boarding the airliners on Martin's ramp.

Check it out, folks. There is a whole new opportunity out there and it's good business. What do the airlines need on your airport? Can you pump their fuel, tote their luggage, tow their aircraft or provide backup maintenance?

I know one sharp FBO manager who used airline maintenance contracts to provide a raise for all his mechanics. The airlines are happy, the mechanics are happy, and the manager is happy.

Go for it. It's out there.

Some words of caution:

First, don't spend any big bucks or hire new crews until you see the *written* contract, which will come down from the big boy's legal department. That contract is going to include some words that weren't mentioned when you and your old buddy, the local station manager, discussed this thing.

Also, don't cut any big deals until you've checked with your insurance carrier. The airlines want to reduce their legal liability, and that contract is going to pass some of it along to you. Find out how much it will cost you to cover it. It may be prohibitive. If so, you can go back and renegotiate if you haven't already bought three new fuel trucks and a place at the beach.

Finally, don't get too cocky. Forget the idea that you can charge whatever you want just because your customer has no choice. Remember, you got the business because somebody else once felt that way.

Ralph's Update:

By golly, I think I hit the nail on the head with this one! Seems to me that it has all come true—and it ain't stopped yet.

□□□□

Moontown may not be heaven, but it's close
(Mar/Apr 1987)

Recreational flying is alive and well in Moontown, AL.

Moontown is a beautiful grass strip on Moontown Road northeast of Huntsville. Some folks say there's also a town called Moontown—and even a guy who calls himself the mayor of Moontown—but I've never seen it and can't comment.

Back in the 1970s I put in a short spell helping Stewart Kimmel sell agplanes in Mississippi, and I never fully recovered. To this day, I get an occasional and uncontrollable urge to fly something with a tailwheel, no radios, and no gyros. It's getting harder to scratch that itch each year, as rental aircraft with tailwheels go the way of six-ounce Cokes and young folks who say "sir."

Last fall my tailwheel itch took me to Moontown Airport. Long, long ago, it was the first grass strip I ever landed on, but I hadn't been there in years. Going back was like entering a time warp.

They're a little confused at Moontown. They still think that aviation can be fun.

Buzz and Janie Barton own and operate the airport and the FBO. The security force is a cocker spaniel by the name of Cassidy. Cassidy takes his job seriously and diligently sniffs everything that moves at the airport.

Buzz always wanted to live where his airplane was tied down, so when he retired from his "real" job he bought Moontown, complete with a home by the runway.

He has a funny idea of retirement. Moontown has over 70 based aircraft, and Buzz is on call about 364 days of the year to pump mogas or avgas, jump start anything that has a dead battery, or handprop anything that has no battery at all.

You don't just fly at Moontown, you belong. There's always a group around the table, and you're welcome to tell your favorite lies when your turn comes around. Buzz will hang your personal coffee cup on the wall opposite the sign that says, "If God had intended that man should fly he would have given him wings...or the intelligence to build his own."

There's still a bench at Moontown, and you can sit, watch, and criticize. On a good Saturday you're likely to see most anything. Charlie Lewis just might roll out the prettiest Stearman in the world, or Tina Everett might bring out her daddy's yaller Cub.

Tina is a student pilot, but she flies the Cub like she was born to it, and I guess she was since the Cub has been in the family about as long as she has. When Tina lands, someone on the bench is likely to sigh, "Ain't she pretty?" You never know if he means the Cub or Tina, since they both qualify.

The soaring club may break out the sailplanes, and you can watch the powered aircraft adjust the pattern to fit them in, all with no tower, no radar, and no TCA.

The best popcorn in aviation is served free at Moontown, as is the coffee and, believe it or not, lunch on Saturday. Yes, Virginia, there is a free lunch.

Janie provides sandwich fixings at no charge whatsoever. You have to buy your own soft drink, but whaddaya want for nothing, a free lunch?

The locals didn't grumble too much when Buzz and Janie closed and left town on Christmas Day. When they weren't back by the next morning, however, that was just too much. The customers opened the place up and ran it 'til Buzz and Janie got back that afternoon. Buzz says they did a pretty good business.

I scratch my tailwheel itch with Moontown's Aeronca Champ, complete with built-in euphoria and chronic oil leak. Buzz also rents "modern" airplanes and keeps two flight instructors busy.

All of this seems too good to be true, and I finally just asked Buzz outright if he's making a profit. He assured me that he is. He said it's not a LOT of profit, and I interrupted him before he could explain. I don't want to know.

I'd rather believe he's getting rich, because I think he and Janie deserve it. On the other hand, I guess maybe he is rich. After all, he does exactly what he always wanted, and how many people do you know who can afford that?

Ralph's Update:

Buzz, Janie, and Cassidy are long gone, but Moontown Airport—like the Mississippi River—rolls on. Within just the last year, Burt Rutan spoke at Moontown right after SpaceShipOne flew into outer space. Moontown's annual fly-in got a beautiful write-up in AOPA Pilot *magazine, and I got a great mother-daughter flying story at Moontown for* AOPA Flight Training *magazine. Moontown is still a thriving, fun airport.*

1988

George Bush the Elder was elected president. The summer Olympics were held in Seoul, South Korea, and "Rain Man" won best picture. I saw it, too.

'You got to ride or get rode' (Mar/Apr 1988)

Aviation folks are an independent—if not cantankerous—lot and seldom agree on anything at all. It took us almost half a century to choose the monoplane over the biplane (the ag aviation boys still argue the point), and to this day we can't decide if the wings should be on the top or the bottom.

When all the aviation experts do agree on something, it's probably time to sit up and take note.

All writers brag about their "industry sources." My main man in aviation matters is Bubba Lee Wainwright of Arkadelphia, AL. Bubba Lee owns a fourth interest in a Taylorcraft he and the boys keep tied out at Arkadelphia International (locally known as Talmadge Murphey's ag strip), and he's up on his aviation knowledge.

Awhile back, Bubba Lee said aircraft management will grow and grow fast. "Those management fellers," he said, "handle the headaches of aircraft ownership, leave the owner with the benefits, and save him money to boot. That has just got to grow."

Normally, I just take Bubba Lee's word for it, but this time I didn't have to. In recent months I have spoken for the Aircraft Finance Association, Wisconsin Aviation Trades Association,

Aircraft and Manufacturers Association, and Airworks. I met a lot of experts, including Larry Burian, president of NATA, and Jonathon Howe, president of NBAA.

All of these people—without a single exception that I found—agree with Bubba Lee. Aircraft management *is* growing, is growing faster and will continue to do so.

It makes sense. The airlines use an airplane up to 3,000 hours per year, spreading the fixed costs among many thousands of passengers. General aviation uses the aircraft only a few hundred hours per year, with a single owner quite often paying all of the fixed costs.

The pride of aircraft ownership took a nosedive with the demise of the Investment Tax Credit, but the prestige, comfort, and convenience of private air transportation remain. Aircraft management makes those benefits less expensive and less troublesome. As Bubba Lee would say, "A deal like that is horse high and hog tight. That dog'll hunt."

A year or two from now, you will probably be in one of two positions. You will be doing well in aircraft management yourself, or you will be complaining about the "outsiders" who have gone into that business on your field.

The FBO is the logical choice to manage aircraft. You already have the on-field office, telephone, staff, fuel, maintenance, and knowledge. You also have the right to sit back on your fixed base and do nothing while others grab up the good management contracts. Then, of course, they'll come to you for discounted fuel, maintenance, and storage for their clients.

Bubba Lee said it best, "This is one of them deals where you got to ride or get rode."

$$****$$

I teach an aviation management course, and we cover all of the major technological breakthroughs in aviation history: the Wright Whirlwind engine, gyro compass, weather radar, turbine engine, and the sausage biscuit.

Dave Naumann—who used to run a shiptight FBO charter department and now runs a Fortune 500 flight department—taught me about airborne biscuits.

Dave puts sausage biscuits on board early morning Navajo flights. "In the Navajo," he said, "we can get the big boss to Atlanta for a morning meeting. If he wanted to sleep 30 minutes longer, we'd have to spend millions more for a jet—*or* put sausage biscuits on board so he can eat breakfast enroute."

That's the way Dave flies. He knows that his real job is taking care of people, not equipment. He rents cars, hails cabs, totes bags, and calls ahead for catering. He works at it. One customer, accustomed to riding in King Airs, flew with Dave for many trips and never learned that the Navajo wasn't pressurized.

Dave's theory is simple: The airlines have bigger, usually faster, airplanes. The only thing we have to offer is better personal service. If we don't provide that, we have no right to exist.

Ralph's Update:

Again, this worked out to be mostly right, except that I still did not anticipate the amazing growth of fractional ownership, which became the big news in aircraft management. Dave Naumann moved up from Navajos and flies corporate jets—is, in fact, a corporate aviation department head. He still works like the dickens at customer service.

〰 〰 〰 〰

Hood's Laws: Let the seller beware! (Jul/Aug 1988)

Recently, I spent a day in court with an FBO who was trying to collect a big bundle owed for charter services.

I can't confirm this, but I'd bet that bad debts have hurt FBOs as much as any other plague short of the federal guvmint. I, therefore, from the kindness of my heart, provide the industry with Hood's Laws of Credit, developed at great expense and pain over the years:

● Any man who brags about his money and his sex life the first time you meet him is a bad credit risk. I don't know if this law applies to women as well but will be happy to research the issue upon request.

● All high rollers are suspect. This particularly applies to charter customers.

● Watch anyone who doesn't haggle over price on large purchases. Most successful people are smart enough to haggle. The con man, on the other hand, can readily agree to any price, since he's not going to pay it anyway.

● Beware the eternal optimist who *always* brags that "Business is great!" Good businesspeople tend to talk about how tough business is, not how easy. If the customer says business is "like stealing candy from a baby," be careful. You might be the baby.

● Watch the charter customer who keeps your pilots in five-star hotel rooms. Bob Hudgens taught me this one. I didn't believe him at first but must now admit that I've never, ever seen an exception to this rule.

● Be wary of a new customer who starts chartering a whole lot all at once. This is a tough one, because you're so delighted to find such a customer. They're not all bad, but proceed with caution.

● The con man, when pressed with a bill, will try to convince you that the bill is not a problem; he's going to pay you as soon as _____ (fill in the blank); he's going to do twice as much business with you next month; and, thanks to his recommendation, Lee Iacocca will be doing a lot of business with you, too. The implication is that only a fool would bother him with this piddlin' little bill right now, just before the good times start to roll. There are a million variations to this theme, and FBOs have fallen for every one of them.

● Cast a jaundiced eye upon those who charter primarily to resort/gambling spots. Those who can afford to charter are usually hardworking folks. If the boss plays daily, who minds the store? If nobody minds the store, where'll the money come from to pay your bill?

● This is the biggy: Beware of any customer who, at any time, for any reason, wants you to vary from your normal payment schedules. If the customer is so strong, how come he/she needs special handling?

Ralph's Update:

When it comes to getting response, this column was one of my top three since 1986. One FBO wrote, "I have lost money by breaking every one of those rules." This column was reprinted on airports around the country. Looking back on it, I wouldn't change a single one of the rules. If I was writing it today, the only change I'd make is the substitution of Bill Gates' name for Iacocca's.

〰 〰 〰 〰

Three FBOs caught my attention in September... (Nov/Dec 1988)

I phoned Rhoades Aviation in Columbus, IN, one day and talked to a woman named Callie. (Back before the feminists taught me better, I would have called Callie a "young lady." Being now enlightened, I'll call her a woman.)

I asked Callie if it was possible to rent a car at her airport at 2:00 p.m. that Saturday. She said it was not but asked me to hang on. I did, and she came back shortly to say it was all worked out. A car would be waiting upon my arrival.

Callie was as good as her word.

I flew into AMR Flight Service Center, Birmingham, AL, late one afternoon to give a speech at the civic center. What to do? Rent a motel room just to take a shower or give the speech dirty (not the same as giving a dirty speech)?

Neither choice was necessary. John McCrainey of AMR offered the use of their charter department's shower, and I appreciated it. I'm almost ashamed to admit it, but we bought only seven gallons of avgas. We did tip the lineman.

Callie at Rhoades and John at AMR both went out of their way to serve the customer. The customer appreciates it.

Then there was the "Mystery FBO." That name has been changed to protect the guilty.

You'd recognize the name of the Mystery FBO's airport. It's a busy place and you'd love to have an FBO there. You might also recognize the name of the FBO.

I was driving a rental car that day, far from home in a strange city. I stopped by the FBO to get a motel recommendation and just to see the FBO operation.

Now I'm not the grand old man of aviation but, dadgummit, I have been on a few airports in my life and claim to know something about finding the FBO.

I went to the wrong building. Twice. I had to ask for directions. Twice.

Once I found the place, there were no parking signs, so I just stuck the car in the only spot I could find.

Out front they fueled heavy iron.

Indoors was, as my mother would say, "just plumb tacky." There was a dingy, dirty look throughout the place.

The bathroom was out in the hangar, and that's where it belonged. It was too dirty to put indoors. The route to it would scare a junkyard dog.

Out front they were pumping fuel faster than you could sell tickets to see the reincarnation of Elvis.

Inside, a lovely little lady (forgive me, feminists, but "lovely little woman" just doesn't sound right.) followed the signs to the bathroom. When she opened the door and saw it led to the hangar, she turned to me and asked, "Is the restroom really out there?"

Outside, they fueled the big airplane the little lady rode in on.

The pay phone was adorned with graffiti, and the handpiece recalled everything you learned about germs in eighth grade health class.

As I talked on that pay phone, a pilot type—complete with epaulets—glanced at me and at his watch. Perhaps, I thought, he thinks I'm his passenger. Then it dawned on me: There was only one pay phone. I hurriedly got off, explaining that I didn't realize this was the only pay phone. "Yes," he said, "and we buy enough fuel here every month to pay for a dozen phones."

I didn't know we had FBOs like that at busy airports. I was ashamed for our industry.

In case you're wondering, no, I will NOT identify the FBO UNLESS the management of the Mystery FBO itself calls.

If the shoe fits, call me at 256-881-2907. I'll be honest with you.

In the meantime, thanks again, Callie and John.

Ralph's Update:

Funny, but all of the questions about this column were about the bad FBO, rather than the two good ones. First, people asked if all of those bad things really happened during one short visit to one FBO. Yep, they really did. I didn't make up a single thing. Second, people wanted to know if the mystery FBO ever called to ask if they were the bad FBO. No, they never did, even though the column included several hints—particularly the restroom in the hangar. (Several good FBOs did call, fearful that I had caught them on a bad day.) By the way, I have been back to the mystery FBO several times since then, and am happy to report that it is much improved.

≈ ≈ ≈ ≈

More *Hood's Laws*: A guide for the conventioneer (Conv Issue 1988)

We attend conventions to buy, sell, learn, network, or all of the above. "Hood's Laws" have been developed, tried, and tested over the years to help you get the most from your convention:

● Never get in someone else's car and ride farther from your hotel than you are willing to walk back.

● If you try to party with all of your customers (or vendors) you will earn both a world-class hangover and a reputation as a drunk.

● Show up early for the first meeting each day. It impresses everyone, even if you skip later meetings.

● Eat breakfast in the coffee shop from 6 'til 9 each morning. Many of the industry's hardest-working people will be there, and they will assume you are one of them. You just might cut a deal over breakfast.

● Take a nap every afternoon. Most of us can't work all day and all night—we're not used to it. (My ex-bosses might be surprised to learn I was napping on company time, but I claim it was a good investment.)

● Wear your name tag on the RIGHT side, not the left. During a handshake your right side moves toward the other person, the left side moves away. Many eagle-eyed pilots wear bifocals and we will appreciate your help.

● Before you rent a car, check on parking fees at the hotel. Chances are you could charter Air Force One cheaper than you can park a Honda.

● Never enter an argument that involves a drunk, especially if you're the drunk.

● Around the corner from expensive hotels there is often a deli that sells corned beef on rye for $3.95. Find it.

****

Conventions have been a big part of my life for more than two decades now, and many highlights linger in my mind:

Meeting Chuck Yeager at the Piper booth.

Watching—at NATA in 1973—as one man changed the course of the FARs. The feds wanted a new rule, and one charter operator stood up and changed their mind with a clear statement of logic and fact. I was impressed. Still am.

Learning—at NATA in 1981—that every GADO in the world was interpreting an FAR differently from our GADO, and having an Oklahoma City big shot tell me quietly that he would "take care of it." A few weeks later it was, indeed, taken care of.

Winning a Staggerwing Beech print by Douglas Ettridge. I am looking at it right now, even as I type.

Being kissed by Miss America. Okay, so she was an EX-Miss America, it was just a peck on the cheek, and my wife was with us. I don't care. She HAD BEEN Miss America, she DID kiss me, and I'm taking full credit for it.

Meeting Maureen O'Hara. Her autograph is on my wall, taped to the plaque given to me at that convention.

Speaking for five minutes at SEATA in 1978. Thanks to that five minutes I was invited to emcee NATA three years running, and that started my speaking career.

And, recently, doing something I've always wanted to do. At a black-tie banquet the main course was truck-tire tough. I attacked it from two directions, then gave up, left the table, went down the stairs, out the door and around the corner to that deli mentioned above. There I got the corned beef on rye for $3.95, took it back to the banquet, and ate it in full view of all present. The fellow across the table offered me $20 for that sandwich. I turned him down.

Most importantly, I remember all of those times that I sat up in surprise during a speech or seminar and said to myself, "I never thought of it that way." When you get right down to it, that's why we go. To learn from and share with each other, so we can go back to our town and our market with a new perspective.

Ralph's Update:

Six months after this column I spoke for Superior Air Parts in Dallas. At the luncheon, after everyone else had been served a fine steak, I had been served nothing. Finally, one of those highly dignified waiters, complete with white cloth napkin over one forearm, brought me a plate containing a Styrofoam container. "Mr. Hood," he said, "this is 'specially for you." Inside was a corned beef on rye. We all laughed, then the waiter tried to take the sandwich and bring a steak. I wasn't having it. I kept the sandwich and ate it with pleasure.

1989

Helluva year! Tiananmen Square become known to the world. San Francisco had another earthquake and—wonder of wonders—the Berlin Wall came down. "Driving Miss Daisy" won best picture. I not only saw it, I loved it. One of my favorite pictures of all time.

On the road in Monroe and Bakersfield (Jan/Feb 1989)

Monroe, LA, ain't a bad place to wait out a thunderstorm.

Thunder and lightning woke me in the Holiday Inn about 4 that morning, and it was worth getting up just to see the sound and light show. God, when He (or She, I don't want to start any fights) wants to, can make Disney look like a sissy.

The lights were off all over town. I opened the curtains wide but couldn't see a light anywhere.

Have you ever tried to shower in total darkness? It's not that bad unless you drop the soap.

I was washing my face when the phone rang. I leaped from the shower, eyes squinched tight and fumbled my way to the phone. Whoever it was hung up. I cussed, wiped off my face, and opened my eyes.

Every light in the room was on. The curtains were still wide open.

A steady stream of cars drove through the dark parking lot outside my window. Some honked, presumably at me.

I was embarrassed. Fat folks look funny naked.

The storms still raged when I got to the Monroe airport, so I did the same thing I did when thunderstorms caught me there 15 years ago. I waited.

The FBO, Fleeman Aviation, is a pleasant place, with ample waiting room, telephones, and free popcorn.

Monroe is in cotton country and Fleeman uses local color in an attractive and profitable manner. They sell cotton souvenir items. That way the customer pays for the color and Fleeman makes a profit on it. Makes sense to me.

Fleeman is fortunate in that the terminal, including rental cars and restaurant, is right next door. It's not even a long walk.

Monroe has the only airport restaurant I've seen in years that I'd eat at voluntarily.

When the weather finally got up to my cowardly standards, a tire was soft. A Fleeman lineman filled it, then tried to turn down my tip. I forced it on him. He deserved it.

Fleeman Aviation represents our industry well.

Million Air, Bakersfield, CA, is another nice FBO. I was only there for a few minutes but was impressed.

Bakersfield lies in the San Joaquin Valley, normally referred to as the BEAUTIFUL San Joaquin Valley and rightfully so.

This just has to be one of the world's most interesting places. There are oil, cotton, almonds, grapes, and citrus fruit there. The California Raisins of TV fame come from there.

The area has been the inspiration for at least two top country songs: "I'll Never Swim Kern River Again," by Merle Haggard, and "Streets of Bakersfield" by Buck Owens and Dwight Yoakam.

As near as I remember, Million Air was not taking advantage of any of this fascinating local color. While writing this column, I got to worrying about my memory, so I called Million Air, long distance.

A pleasant fellow answered, and I asked if they had souvenirs of the area on sale. He said, "No sir, but if you can tell me when you're flying in, we can arrange to have some here for you."

That, folks, is a customer-oriented fellow. But I still wonder if Million Air wouldn't come out ahead having those souvenirs on hand all the time.

Ralph's Update:

My friend, high-tech aerial photographer Bill Broadway, regularly photographs a paper company stockpile in the Monroeville area. He says the airport restaurant is still a great place to eat. Amazing, I first ate there in the early 1970s! (One word of caution: If you eat at the counter, watch that first step when you get off the stool. It's a surprise.)

"How could that happen, Daddy?" (Mar/Apr 1989)

College daughter Melanie has a best friend we shall call Susan (not her real name, but it'll do). Janice was an acquaintance of Melanie's and a very good friend of Susan's.

We refer to Janice in the past tense because Janice rode in a light aircraft recently, and Janice died in the crash.

These things do happen. I know that and so do you. But I couldn't explain it to Melanie.

The gossip was that the airplane ran into a thunderstorm, and Melanie's question was simple enough. "How," she asked, "could that happen, Daddy?"

Melanie and Susan didn't understand how a little airplane could accidentally run into a big thunderstorm. I wanted to explain, so I did a little research.

According to my experts, this was an old story: Low-time VFR pilot continues into IFR weather. As Paul Harvey would say, you know the rest of the story.

I explained that to Melanie, and she had another simple question. "Why," she wanted to know, "would anybody do that?"

Why indeed?

I decided a few years back that I no would longer defend the indefensible in aviation, so I answered frankly. "For the same reason," I said, "that some people drive drunk."

Another pilot took exception. "The drunk driver," he said, "acted immorally. The pilot had an accident."

I disagree. The VFR pilot has a moral obligation to stay clear of clouds. And those who teach flying have a moral obligation to teach the responsibilities of flight along with the freedoms.

Some say you can't teach a proper attitude. Again, I disagree. Twenty-five years of education have, for example, certainly changed America's attitude toward smoking and smokers.

For decades, we have mouthed that, "The drive to the airport is the most dangerous part of flying." For business and pleasure flying, statistics prove otherwise. We can change that, but only if we produce pilots with responsible attitudes.

****

Now, for the good news…

Simple aircraft can provide sophisticated benefits.

I had a speech in Indiana last week and then another in Florida.

You can get from Huntsville, AL, to Montgomery, IN, via airline and rental car, but it'd be tough on a fat fellow with a thin wallet.

First, you'd fly to Nashville, Memphis, or Atlanta, then connect to Indianapolis, Louisville, or Evansville, from whence you'd drive a couple of hours to the final destination. Add a few hours of waiting for airlines, rental cars, and baggage, and you've got a grueling trip with a high total cost.

Instead, we flew a basic airplane (180 hp, fixed gear, and fixed prop) to Indiana in 2 hours 13 minutes. I say "we" because fellow pilot and friend, Jack Montgomery, went along just for the fun of it. You can't do that on the airlines, but then who would want to?

The folks at the Daviess County, IN, airport proved—once again—that good service can be found at little airports, and southern hospitality can be found north of the Mason-Dixon Line.

Next morning, instead of the drive, fly, connect, drive routine, we flew to Jacksonville, FL, stopping for lunch with my mother in Brunswick, GA, where, again, FBO service was good.

Craig Air Center in Jacksonville treated us well also, and my friend was highly impressed when FBO personnel Mike Muchmore and Dave Ekey recognized me and bragged on this magazine. Thanks, Mike and Dave.

The flight back was pleasant, and the entire trip cost very little more than roundtrip airfare to Jacksonville alone.

That's utility.

Ralph's Update:

I still get a little upset thinking about Melanie's questions. She had grown up around airplanes but just wasn't aware of this aspect of aviation. On the other hand, memories of the Alabama, Indiana, Florida trip still bring great satisfaction. Fuel has climbed and airfares dropped since that trip, so it is harder today to beat the airlines on price. Still, the little airplane can often make possible a profit-making trip that would not have been possible on the airlines.

Learning from those who have the best job in the world (Jun 1989)

I wonder if anyone could possibly estimate the total positive effect of 40 good managers. I've worked under a few good managers, and every single day I remember—and use—at least one valuable lesson learned from those few mentors.

Among other things, I have learned that:

The crooked manager cannot teach ethics, the ethical manager seldom has to. If the manager is cheating the insurance company, the bank, the telephone company, and the customers, chances are the employees are cheating the manager.

The manager with values faces far fewer decisions than the manager with none. The ethical manager decides once and for all that the company will be run honestly. That decision made, the manager's time is devoted to running the company, rather than to deciding which corner will be cut and which sleazy deal will be accepted.

The customer is NOT always right. The customer who wants to charge sunglasses to his company's gas account is wrong, as is the customer who wants an overweight charter flight. The pilot who wants money "under the table" for bringing his company's aircraft to your shop is wrong. The customer who wants the aircraft salesman to find him an airplane "on the side," cutting the FBO out of the deal, is wrong.

The manager's habits—good and bad—will be picked up by the employees.

Some business is simply not worth having. This includes most twin-engine aircraft rental, pilot service in strange aircraft, and renting any airplane to any customer that thinks your rules are silly. There are exceptions, but usually the exception is a mistake.

You don't override pilots on weather or mechanics on maintenance. What is even harder to remember: You don't override your own rules on extending credit.

A crook is generally better at cheating you than you are at catching him. After all, that's his job. The moral is obvious: Do as little business with known cheats as possible and never on any terms other than your own.

The person who wants you to take this particular deal at a loss, in order to get a lot more business in the future, is going to want you to lose money on the future business, too.

The three most important things about used aircraft are: 1) maintenance; 2) maintenance; and, 3) has that airplane been taken care of?

The person who is going to make you rich, ain't.

Everyone wants to feel important. The good manager helps them do so.

People do what you expect only if you inspect, but you must do it with respect. (Study this one a few times. It makes more sense the longer you look at it.)

Drug dealers tend to avoid airports and FBOs that are known to be rigidly honest and hang around those that aren't.

Everybody—not just New York's Mayor Koch—wants to know the answer to the all-important question, "How am I doing?"

It is easy to figure out ahead of time exactly what your competition will do; just figure out what you most hope they will NOT do.

The customer is the ONLY person who brings money INTO the FBO. All others—fuel companies, parts suppliers, FAA, tax collectors, employees—take money OUT. Therefore, the customer pays for everything. Wages, taxes, damaged equipment, mistakes of management, and employees are all paid for by the customer. Any ideas to the contrary are false.

Isolation is expensive and easily arrived at in this industry. Generally, the FBO has few local competitors and tends to measure him/herself against those few. Customers, on the other hand, generally visit many FBOs on a regular basis and measure you against those. The good manager will know how the FBO compares nationally, not just locally.

A good manager has the best job in the world. A poor manager has the worst.

Ralph's Update:

If anything, I believe all of this more strongly today than I did in 1989. I learned the caution about dealing with crooks from the late Bob Hudgens, Montgomery (Alabama) Aviation. We were considering a strange deal from a shady character. Hudgens said, "Look, we know the guy is a crook, let's turn it down." I, younger and more foolish, asked, "But how could he cheat us on this deal?" I can hear Hudgens' answer to this day. "I don't know, and you don't know, but we haven't been lying awake at night trying to figure out how to screw us. This guy has." We didn't take the deal, and I never forgot the advice.

Marketing, hell! Let's sell something! (Oct 1989
Marketing 101)

There are a thousand and two definitions of marketing, one of which is: "Marketing—a high-tech word used when trying to avoid that dirty old low-tech word, 'selling.'"

Most aviation folks are scared to death of the word "sell." How many times have you heard otherwise intelligent people brag about that? "I can't sell. I can do a lot of things, but I just flat can't sell anything."

"Selling" has a pushy sound to it. I know businesspeople—retailers—who live in absolute fear that the customer will think someone is trying to "sell" them something.

"Marketing," on the other hand, has a genteel ring to it. It smacks of college degrees, boardrooms, and worldwide advertising campaigns. Nothing pushy about that word, no sir.

Nobody wants to be a salesperson. The pushiest companies—those selling encyclopedias, magazines, and/or pots and pans door to door—have long since learned this and no longer even advertise for salespeople. Instead, they recruit "Marketing Specialists."

We live in fear that people will "mistakenly" think we are trying to sell them something. We even say it: "Now, I'm not trying to sell you anything…"

Like hell we aren't.

Marketing may represent the white knight of business, but let's not forget for a second that the end goal of marketing is to sell something to somebody.

This issue contains marketing ideas, plans, and campaigns, none of which will work unless somebody—the somebody who actually deals with the customer—is prepared to sell something.

You can market your fuel service with national advertising, direct mail, and follow-me trucks, but it's all wasted unless your line and front-desk people understand that you are in the business to *sell* fuel.

True story: "Why," I once asked an FBO front-desk manager, "do you let that one corporate jet park up front every week instead of out on the ramp with everybody else?" Her answer was classic: "Because they like to park up front, and because this is their second stop every week. They could top off at their first stop, but they don't; they top off here because we let them park up front."

The woman was selling fuel.

Marketing can increase the general aviation pie. But you won't get your share of the pie unless your CFIs and charter pilots can sell.

True story: A customer called an FBO charter department with a simple question: "Do you have a DC-3?" The simple answer was, "No, we don't." But the charter manager was a salesperson. He didn't give the simple answer, he asked another simple question: "When do you need a DC-3?" That question reaped a nice profit on $1,300,000 in brokered DC-3 charter business during the next year.

Marketing attracts prospects. Selling turns them into customers. Why spend the money on the former if you aren't prepared to do the latter?

Do you plan to market flight training? For goodness' sake, if you're going to make the effort and spend the money to attract the prospects, take the time to *sell* (there's that word again) the program to your CFIs, front desk, bookkeeping, and line people. Make sure they understand and agree with your goals, that they know the type of prospect you expect to attract, and what it will take to *sell* that prospect.

Marketing without selling is like hunting big game with an empty rifle. You're going through the motions, but you're not going to put any meat on the table.

Ralph's Update:

Lord, y'all, I wouldn't change a word. I've spent a good part of my life trying to sell this concept. Mostly I had but limited success, particularly when it came to selling flight instruction. I remain convinced that flight instruction is a very sellable product, because I have seen selling it succeed every time it was tried. Problem is, it isn't tried often enough.

1990

We went to war with Iraq and the feds passed the Americans With Disabilities Act. "Dances With Wolves" won best picture. Five years later, when I was on a program with Dick Rutan, I told a story about riding in the back of a Piper Pacer with a live shark. Ever since, Dick has called me Flies With Sharks. Makes me feel important.

My box runneth over with junk mail (Jan/Feb 1990)

Surely I will dwell in the house of catalogs forever.

During the recent holiday season, I received brochures and catalogs extolling the benefits of fruit from the states of Washington, Florida, and New York. According to additional sales literature, everyone on my Christmas list sincerely desired steaks from Omaha, live lobsters from Maine, books from a number of states, and grapefruit from the Indian River.

Still others touted fudge from Grandma's kitchen, cheese from Wisconsin, and live cactuses (cacti?) from New Mexico.

I could—the literature said—complete all of my Christmas shopping by telephone, fax (that was new in 1989), or mail, with a little help from MasterCard, Visa, or American Express.

The aviation industry was in on this. I got catalogs from a variety of aviation mail-order firms, reminding me that the pilot on my gift list would love the latest headset, radio, carbon monoxide tester, or relief tube.

Come to think of it, it seems to me that every retailer in the world tried to sell me something, with one notable exception. Not a single FBO tried to sell me a single thing for the folks on my Christmas list.

That seems a bit odd.

I read and hear that the aviation industry is not yet out of the doldrums, yet no FBO tried to sell me a private pilot course for my children or a pinch hitter course for my wife. No FBO suggested that I give my aviation friends a gift certificate good for wash job, barf bag, or special aviation flashlight.

Maybe I'm considered to be a poor prospect. On the other hand, Harry and David (the folks from whom I bought the Christmas fruit in 1988), sold my name in 1989 to the people who sell candy, cheese, and steak. How come no FBO has me on a list?

Sporty's sure has me on a list, as do a myriad of other aviation catalog houses. It works, too. Just recently I ordered a foolproof, self-sealing, hand-held, corrosion-resistant portable urinal for $29.95. Surely anyone who will pay that much for a pot to you-know-what in is worthy of a sales effort.

Yet not a single FBO has me on a mailing list. It's enough to make you wonder if a single FBO HAS a mailing list.

Walk into any department store, drugstore, hardware, or even food store toward the end of any year. The Christmas displays go up as the Halloween displays come down. Look in any direction for something being sold as the perfect Christmas gift. Do you realize plumbers advertise FAUCETS as gifts? And people BUY them?

Walk into any FBO during the same time period and you'll see fuel prices, solo and dual rental rates, shop rates, and not a single partridge in a pear tree.

This is a year-round phenomenon. So far this year, someone or other has tried to sell me cemetery lots, life and health insurance, retirement plans, and additive-free foods, all for the safety and security of my family; but no FBO has tried to sell me recurrency training, which would indeed add to the safety and security of my family.

During the last year I bought—or influenced the decision to buy—charts, logbooks, Stormscopes, lorans, and one airplane. How come no FBO tried to sell me anything all year?

I got a monthly bill from one FBO, and I can't recall that they included a single piece of sales literature in one of those bills.

I'm not suggesting that you put the charter pilot in a Santa Claus suit this year, or add a toy department to the shop, but it does seem to me that we could swap of lot of ho-hum for a little bit of ho-ho during December.

And surely the FBO could sell SOMETHING extra during the holidays!

I mean, for crying out loud, why didn't SOMEBODY tell my wife that I wanted an aerobatic, single pilot, transoceanic SST for Christmas?

Ralph's Update:

After this column was published, Hal Shevers, founder of Sporty's Pilot Shop, wrote my wife a funny note trying to sell her an SST for my birthday. One FBO has tried to sell me something every year since this column came out. That's Tom Peterson, Petecraft Aviation of Plains, GA. Congratulations, Tom, you're still the only one!

✈ ✈ ✈ ✈

Thriving on chaos (Mar/Apr 1990)

Every FBO manager, at every level, should read Tom Peters' book, "Thriving on Chaos." Correction: Every FBO manager should STUDY this book in detail and at length.

If you attended the 1989 NATA convention, you were offered a free copy of "Chaos" from Aviall. If you didn't get one, it's well worth buying (Aviall's were all snapped up quickly).

"Chaos" wasn't written specifically for FBOs, but could have been. I certainly can't cover the whole book in this space, but would like to mention two ideas that seem particularly pertinent to our industry.

Idea Number One: Get used to change.

Change is not only not going away, it's going to come faster.

Lord knows we've seen a lot of change in this industry. Many of us remember the prime interest rate doubling in one year and aircraft sales dropping 87.5 percent in five years (after which it got BAD). How many of us have wondered out loud if things will ever get back to "normal?"

Peters says not only will things never get back to normal, but there AIN'T no more normal (he didn't put it exactly that way, but you get the idea). "Normal," according to Peters, is a thing of the past. Not only will things never be like they WERE, they won't even stay the way they ARE.

Change, says Peters, is now normal. It is no longer enough to merely EXPECT change, but we must see change as opportunity rather than obstacle. Successful businesspeople of the future will thrive on change; will look for opportunity in change; will say, "This is changing. How can I profit from the change? What new needs does the change create for customers? How can I fill those needs?"

We have all seen aviation people fight change. The round engine would dominate forever, the turbine engine was a fad, the Stearman would always be the best ag aircraft, weather radar would never catch on, the Twin Beech would forever remain the flagship of the corporate fleet, and only sissies used autopilots. All that seems silly now, but which of today's "facts" will look silly ten, five, or even one year from now? Who will profit from the new ideas? Who will lose?

Idea Number Two: Sell value added.

The successful business of the future will sell on the basis of "value added."

Value added means that you take a "seemingly similar" product, make it different by adding value, then sell the difference. (This is in my words, not Peters'. His words say we must quit selling commodities and start selling products with value added. Either way, he is right.)

Aviation fuel is a commodity, much as wheat is a commodity. In the eyes of the customer (and nobody else's eyes matter at all), wheat is wheat and avfuel is avfuel. How then, does one compete? On price, scream many. Nay, nay, says Peters. One competes by adding value.

Avfuel is a commodity, but avfuel PLUS service is a product. The service is the added value. One competes by providing unique service, better service, faster service, cleaner service, and/or more pleasant service.

Incidentally, Peters' research indicates this value-added concept is most highly rewarded in fields where the product itself is most like a commodity, in other words, most similar.

Anyone who doubts this, just take a look as you travel from one airport to another. I submit to you that the FBO providing the best service—where there IS an FBO providing good service—is more than likely selling the most fuel, often at a higher price.

And remember, the customer's definition of good service is the ONLY one that counts. Period. It matters not what you think, what I think, or what your chief lineperson thinks. The customer is both judge and jury. Period.

There's more in "Chaos"—a lot more. Peters calls "Chaos" a handbook for management revolution. I have a feeling he's right, and we're all going to participate in this revolution, ready or not.

Ralph's Update:

I can't believe I wrote all of the above without pointing out that the airlines were at the time busily ignoring very important changes in their industry. Today we see them suffering greatly for their failure to change. Also, at the time of this column I was a devout believer in selling "value added" instead of price. I have come to believe that you can't sell value added INSTEAD of price, you must sell both. A sale always gets down to price. The goal is to sell value added first so that by the time it does get down to price the customer wants your value added enough that he/she will pay you a little bit more to get it.

✈ ✈ ✈ ✈

Let me risk the wrath of the industry... (May/Jun 1990)

By saying it up front, out loud and in public: I believe in user fees! But there is a condition.

Basically speaking, I do believe that them what uses should pay. Free enterprise works that way and works well. Shouldn't guvmint copy free enterprise to the extent possible? But—that one all-important condition must be met.

It's hard to tell what is really important to folks when they are spending other people's money. For example, I don't buy luxury cars. It's not worth the extra money to me. But if *you're* going to buy me a car, I'll dang sure take a Cadillac, Mercedes, or BMW. I can even put up a good argument that I need such a fine car. I wouldn't spend my money on one, but I'll take two or three if it's your money.

When my kids were young, we made them pay half of all trips taken by their church, scout troop, band, and other groups. That was a user fee. It didn't save us a lot of money per trip, but it sure did cut down on the number of trips. We found out if it was all our money, every trip that came along was crucially important. If they didn't get to go it would warp their personalities, and they would never be president or play the violin. If, however, it was half their money, they decided some of those trips really weren't all that important.

Insurance companies know that we take better care of our property when the policy has a deductible. After an accident, we shop better for repairs if a coinsurance clause requires us to pay a percentage of the cost. We even do this when our personal health is insured. It's human nature.

Maybe all guvmint benefits should require a user fee. It worries me that there is no charge to enter the Smithsonian Institution. They even check your coat free! It's not really free, of course, the taxpayers pay for it. Does it really make sense for a working stiff in Seattle—who has never been to Washington, D.C.—to pay for me to see Jackie Kennedy's dress and Michael Jackson's glove at the Smithsonian?

User fees remind us that there ain't no free lunch, and we need that reminder. If we think it's "free," why take care of it? Why use it efficiently? Why use it wisely? Why use it sparingly?

Be honest now: Wouldn't you mail more stuff if it were "free?" Of course you would. So would I. I might even mail as much as my congressman, for whom it *is* free.

I believe in user fees. And, yes, I believe in user fees for aviation. But there is a condition that makes it all possible.

I think airline passengers should help pay for the system, and I think we should, too. Again, I don't see why the working stiff who never flies should foot the bill for my flying, be it business or pleasure. I've heard all the arguments to the contrary, and I still think them that uses should pay.

On the other hand…

User fees don't work unless there is an honest party to hold the money. There has to be an honest person—or group of persons—to whom you can entrust the money. There has to be an honest party to hold the money and to be sure it is spent for the purpose for which it was collected. That is essential to the concept of user fees.

We have aviation user fees right now, mostly in the form of fuel taxes. This is no new concept. Unfortunately, we do not have an honest party to hold and spend the money as promised.

The guvmint told us that we must pay our share. I agreed. The guvmint collected the money from us and from millions of airline passengers. But the guvmint refuses—repeat, refuses—to use the money for the purpose for which it was collected. That's dishonest. If you or I did that, the guvmint would lock us up, and should.

Does anyone, anywhere, still doubt that the guvmint is using the Aviation Trust Fund to make the deficit appear less odious? Let me remove all doubt. I have a letter from my congressman in which he explains that this is exactly what the guvmint is doing.

Private enterprise is doing its job. Since deregulation, there are more airline flights, more airplanes, and a better safety record. Fares have gone up less than half as much as inflation. Yet we have not built a major new airport in this country since DFW. Still the guvmint refuses to spend our money as promised.

Yes, I believe in aviation user fees. I have paid aviation user fees. I got took. I oppose additional user fees until I become convinced that an honest party exists to hold the money bag. What would so convince me? Simple. Just spend my Aviation Trust Fund as promised.

There are honest bookies in my town. You can trust them with your money. I trust insurance companies, banks, Las Vegas dealers, and used car salesmen to hold my money and use it as promised. Unfortunately, I cannot so trust the United States guvmint.

Ralph's Update:

Lord a mercy, y'all, this was in 1990, and I was still writing about user fees in AIRPORT BUSINESS *in 2005. The guvmint finally did spend our Aviation Trust Fund, although not exactly as promised. When this was written, DFW was indeed the newest major airport in our land; today DFW is the second newest. We did build one—but only one—major airport since then—in Denver. As Morgan Freeman's character said in the movie "Driving Miss Daisy" "Things ain't changed all THAT much."*

♩ ♩ ♩ ♩

Two of the best bits of business advice I ever received... (Jul/Aug 1990)

1) Concentrate on your current job.
2) Hone that sucker.

That first bit came in 1964 from Dean Skadberg, my first boss on my first "real" job after college, the very first day on that job.

I was straight out of college, I had a sales job with a Fortune 500 company, and I was right impressed with myself. At graduation they told us we represented the future of the world, and I believed it.

I showed up that first day full of vim and vigor, eager to take my place as a world leader. I asked questions about promotions, getting ahead, and moving up. I didn't intend to remain at the bottom long. Hadn't the graduation speaker said we were the cream of the crop?

After a few minutes, Dean Skadberg explained things. "Ralph," he said, "we hired you to sell our product. The best way to get ahead in this company is to forget about promotions and just concentrate on your current job."

Dean Skadberg has lived by his own advice, and today his business card reads "Director of Industry Affairs, Procter & Gamble." Dean has never run an FBO, but we could all learn from him.

Small FBOs often spend great amounts of management effort trying to become big FBOs. Business guru Tom Peters says this is because we were all raised to believe that big is good, bigger is better, and biggest is best. (Peters also says it ain't true, and never was, but that's a different story.)

Dean Skadberg, I think, would say that the small FBO's current job is to run a damned fine small FBO, concentrating on current customers, current facilities, and current markets. I think he would be right.

The second bit of good advice—"hone that sucker"—came from Robert Henry, dean of public speakers in Alabama.

Back in the 1970s I made a few speeches and it went to my head. I loved it. I wanted to do more. I went to Robert Henry for advice, and he asked one big question: "What kind of speaking are you doing?" I assured him I could speak to any group on any subject.

"Boy," Robert drawled, "you listen to me. Forget that stuff about a different speech for every group. You get yourself one good speech and hone that sucker. Give it to anybody who'll listen. Get good at it. Become a professional. Get so good at it that people will pay you for that speech. Then—but only then—you can think about coming up with a second speech."

It was good advice, and it worked for me. That was 12 years ago. I have many different speeches and seminars now, but I honed that first speech for years before I came up with the second one.

How many FBOs leap from one service into another, trying to be all things to all people, expanding into this market and that without becoming truly professional at any?

This issue of *FBO* features two small operators who are concentrating on the job their customers hired them to do. They are, as they used to say where I grew up in Georgia, "tendin' to their business"—their current business. They may become bigger—the best small businesses get the best opportunities to become bigger—but they don't have to. Either way, they will make profits serving the public.

Each of these FBOs has found a niche in the marketplace, one in flight training, the other in aircraft painting. They have become professional at it. They work at it, they are good at it, they profit by it, and they stick with it.

Recently I ate lunch with Don Morrisson, who started out slinging baggage for Ozark and is now TWA's vice president, public affairs. He pointed out that discount airlines tend to do well at first, then fail ignominiously. "They do well," Don said, "as long as they stay in their niche, serving routes where they are needed and have expertise. They fail when they try to expand and compete with big airlines on routes where they aren't needed."

Dean Skadberg, Robert Henry, Don Morrisson, and the two small FBOs in this issue—we can all learn a lot from each of them.

Ralph's Update:

Those two bits of advice are as good today as they were then. Skadberg has since retired to a huge house on top of the hill. Robert Henry stayed on the top of the speaking business until his death a few years ago, and I miss him still. Don Morrisson proved his adaptability by moving his skills and talents to a totally different industry after the demise of TWA, and thrives to this day.

/z /z /z /z

How long since you ate at a truck stop? (Nov/Dec 1990)

Back in the 1960s, I ate at truck stops only late at night, when everything else was closed. They tended toward dirty, noisy, and profane. The food was subsidized by TUMS, Rolaids, and Alka Selzer.

But—to paraphrase Ford commercials—have you driven a truck stop lately?

Back in July, Bill and Betty Whatley (Huntsville Aviation, HSV, AL) and I stopped for lunch at the Flying J Truck Stop on I-75 at Resaca, GA. It wasn't necessarily where we wanted to stop, but we were hungry, it was the only place around, and we decided one more greasy meal wouldn't kill us.

We halfway expected a waitress complete with "Born to Raise Hell" tattoo and Boxcar Willie tee shirt.

We were pleasantly surprised.

Truck stops have come of age. The Flying J was clean, the waitress friendly and tattooless, the food well above average. They weren't into spinach quiche or baked Alaska, but the meat, potatoes and gravy were better than expected, and, for the money, superior to many a meal served at Mr. Marriott's place.

We enjoyed it, and we learned a lot. Frankly, the Flying J could teach us all a thing or two about niche marketing. They know who their customers are and cater to them.

The place is set up for truck drivers. There's a payphone at each booth, so drivers no longer have to stand at a greasy wall phone outside the men's room, nor must they stick close to the phone waiting for their dispatcher to call back. They do their calling right from the booth, while waiting for their meal, and they leave "their" number so the dispatcher can call back during dessert.

Overnight parking is free for Flying J fuel customers, and, when you get ready to leave, they fill your coffee thermos free. Showers are likewise free, as is use of the drivers' lounge with big-screen TV. They have FAX service, a frequent-fueler program, and wire service so drivers can receive funds care of the Flying J. When there's a crowd in the restaurant, drivers are served first.

The Flying J knows that drivers, not truck owners, decide where fuel will be purchased, so they try to please and attract the driver. It makes sense.

More than anything else, the Flying J reminded us of a good FBO, catering to the corporate pilot.

Most of us figured out a good while back that the King Air pilot, not the owner, selects the FBO. That's why smart FBOs compete by providing pilot lounges, health clubs, courtesy cars, and free coffee instead of cut-rate fuel.

Airlines do the same. Frequent-flying programs were designed to benefit the passenger, rather than the company paying for the ticket. Flying J's frequent-fueler program works the same way. The driver uses points to buy personal items.

(The theory can be overdone. Some of us remember when pilots bought stereo sets with Green Stamps earned on the boss's fuel purchases, and many think the airlines have gone too far with frequent-flyer programs. As travel costs climb, many companies are looking harder at these programs. Procter & Gamble, for one, now asks employees to use their "free" travel bonuses for company trips.)

In general, though, it's a good theory, and I wonder if FBOs aren't missing the boat in one area. Are we treating freight pilots with respect proportionate to their fuel purchases? All over the country I see freight pilots adjusting to services designed with the corporate or owner pilot in mind. Sometimes the freight pilot who purchases hundreds of gallons weekly plays second fiddle to the local neurosurgeon who flies his single 100 hours a year.

Over the history of commercial transportation, freight has always become more important with the maturation of each new method of getting from here to there. It happened with ships, trains, highway travel, and airlines; now it's happening to general aviation. Maybe it's time to look at freight pilots with respect, rather than down our noses.

Ralph's Update:

Danged if I don't look like a diamond in a slop jar on this one. Freight hauling is probably the healthiest segment of the airline industry. Many a pilot who looked down on "freight dogs" now wishes he/she had a job with FedEx or one of the other biggies.

✈ ✈ ✈ ✈

How come "marketing" gets so much more attention than "customer service"? (Aug 1990)

We seem to think "marketing" can, in some dignified manner, solve all our problems by supplying a steady stream of new customers. "Customer service," on the other hand, brings to mind hard, never-ending work, dealing with problems, keeping people happy, listening to complaints, and all those other things we have never been able to do as well as we know we should.

We all know that keeping an old customer costs less than finding a new one, but somehow marketing for new customers is more fun than catering to the old ones. There is always the hope that marketing will provide new customers who will appreciate us, pay their bills on time, and never have a problem we can't handle quickly, efficiently, and to their total satisfaction.

As the song says, dream on.

Folks, you can market 'til blue in the face, and at best you're gonna find new customers exactly like the old ones. If you can't keep the old, how're you gonna please the new?

Let's face it: Your product and location are similar to your competitor's, at least in the customer's opinion, and that's the only opinion that matters. Marketing might get new customers to try your FBO, but marketing won't bring 'em back. The new customer is new for only one purchase. After that he is either an old customer or a gone customer.

Chances are you've got your facilities fixed up about as nice as possible, but so does your competitor. So how're you gonna compete? How're you gonna make your product different from the competitor's?

There are only two ways I know of: price and customer service. Customer service works better, lasts longer, and is more profitable.

One thing to remember about customer service: Forget all those old sayings like, "Let a sleeping dog lie," "Don't fix it if it ain't broke," "Leave well enough alone." They won't get the job done. Customer service probably can't be improved until it is measured, and this means you must solicit complaints from the only people who count: your customers. Ask them how you're doing. Make it easy for them to tell you where you're falling short.

Statistics indicate (write me if you want the source) that complaining customers are really saying, "Listen, if I didn't want to do business with you in the future I wouldn't bother telling you about this problem."

A whopping 46 percent of complaining customers come back even if you don't solve their problems. Solve the problems and the figure jumps to somewhere between 54 percent and 70 percent. Solve their problems quickly—in their opinion, not yours—and over 90 percent of complaining customers will return to do business with you. And each one of them will tell five other people how well you handled their complaint.

If you still doubt the benefits of soliciting complaints, pick up any product put out by Procter & Gamble. Somewhere on that product you'll find a toll-free number with the invitation for you to call with "Questions or Comments." People do call by the hundreds of thousands, and Procter & Gamble—one of the best marketing companies in the world—claims a high profit on the cost of the calls.

Customers want to know that your company cares about them and their problems. An irate customer and a drunk are alike in that they both desperately want to be taken very seriously. You should authorize and encourage frontline folks to solve problems on the spot when possible, and to report all other problems to someone who can solve them.

The mere manner of reporting can make a big difference. A line person might say, "I can't do anything about it. Mr. Bigshot is the only person who can, and he's not here." Or, instead, he might say, "Gosh, I'm sorry you are upset. Mr. Bigshot will want to handle this personally. Let me write down all the details so he can take care of this the minute he gets back." What a difference.

Jan Carlzon, the manager who took Scandinavian Airlines from near bankruptcy to high profits in less than two years, measured his assets in satisfied customers, not capital. Marketing will get new customers, but only service brings 'em back.

Ralph's Update:

Obviously, I still believed that value added could be sold instead of price, rather than along with price. The truth is that customer service is very important, and if you don't sell customer service you will sell on price alone. The customer expects to find lower prices at the business with poor service. The same customer expects to find—and is willing to pay—somewhat higher prices at the business with good service.

1991

"Silence of the Lambs" won best picture. I read the book, skipped the picture. The old USSR continued to evolve into something different but nobody seemed to be sure exactly what. Hypertext Transfer Protocol was implemented by the World Wide Web—which had by now been invented by Al Gore—and we still type HTTP today.

"To thine own self be true" (Mar 1991)

This story is more than 20 years old now, so I guess I can muster up the nerve to confess it.

Back in the 1960s I needed to sell my car, which looked better than normal for its high mileage. I had some slick friends who told me to turn back the odometer. "Everybody," they said, "does it. You'd be a fool not to."

I paid $10 to have the odometer turned back. The first prospect quite casually asked, "Is that the true mileage?" The blood rushed from my head, I stammered, stuttered, and, finally, blurted out the lie, "I reckon so."

The next day I paid $10 to have the odometer turned back up to the true mileage.

Getting older has its advantages.

One of the benefits of being at the half-century mark is that most of us old-timers made our ethical decisions—painfully—years ago.

When the questions arise today we don't have to agonize over them. We already know what we're going to do.

At a recent business meeting, a young employee, bright and eager but worried, asked a simple question: "My boss wants me to do it this way. That seems unethical to me. Do you think it's unethical? What should I do?"

To all young employees, I'd say the same thing: Don't rely on me, your boss, or your customers to tell you what's ethical. Instead, decide for yourself who you are, what you stand for, and what is ethical for you. Then stick to your guns. Don't let anyone else set your standards.

This holds particularly true for young pilots. You decide if you're willing to fly this airplane, in this weather, with this load, on this day. Then stick to your guns. Don't let anyone risk your life.

Young technicians, decide for yourselves what you will and won't sign off. Don't let others decide what you will approve.

Salespeople, decide right now if you're going to tell the customer everything you know—good and bad—about every used airplane. Decide for yourself how far you will go to make a sale. Make up your own mind about being honest with the bank when getting a customer financed, or with the insurance carrier when getting one insured.

Front-office people, do you think it's right to charge the pilot's sunglasses to his boss's account, putting them down as fuel? If not, don't do it, regardless of what others are doing.

Is it okay to cheat a little bit on the expense account, lie a little bit to the insurance company, climb through a thin cloud layer on a VFR flight plan? It depends, or should depend, primarily on whom you are and what you believe in rather than what someone else is willing to accept.

As the old saying goes, if you don't stand for something you're likely to fall for anything.

Don't get me wrong. It's good to get advice. To this day, I have friends to call when I'm faced with an ethical decision. They have high standards, and I call to make sure my decisions measure up to their standards. I call them my "board of integrity."

It's sometimes hard to believe that "honesty is the best policy," particularly when you're young and everyone seems to be saying, "To get along, go along."

But integrity does pay. Refuse to "go along" and you may be fired, but it's more likely you'll be promoted over those who do. Tell the truth and you may lose a sale, but your sales career will most likely thrive. Stick to your standards, and you'll find others adapting to you, rather than the other way around. Look around. People of high integrity generally do pretty well in life.

Shakespeare said it best (in "Hamlet"): "This above all: To thine own self be true, and it must follow, as the night the day, thou canst not then be false to any man."

Ralph's Update:

Y'all, I just can't be modest about this one. I get plumb proud all over every time I read. It is flat out good advice, and I'm delighted that I wrote it. So there!

ㅁ ㅁ ㅁ ㅁ

There are times when we just do it better (Apr 1991)

General Aviation has only two functions—business and pleasure—and it's a pleasure to report that GA has really helped my speaking business this year.

Normally, a speaker is delighted to speak for one group on any given day. Thanks to GA, on three different occasions this spring I can speak for two groups in two states on the same day—Alabama and Georgia on February 25, North Carolina and Ohio on March 16, and Wisconsin and Iowa on April 15. The extra jobs thus obtained will increase my little business by 16 percent in one quarter. I appreciate it.

GA's most useful role is doing the job that can't be done any other way, and these trips are perfect examples. In each case GA made it possible to get additional jobs—jobs that absolutely, positively couldn't have been reached by traveling the airlines.

In each case the small extra cost of GA aircraft was overshadowed by the extra revenue derived from the job. In two of the three cases there was no extra cost. GA was cheaper than airfare even if the airlines could have done the job.

Here's the big question: If my little business found three profitable GA trips in three months, how many such trips would a bigger company find? Let's change that. How many such trips SHOULD the bigger company find?

We spotted those trips because we know what GA can do. We can spot the trip situations where GA shines. Can your charter prospect do that? Or does she call for a quote to take one person to Hawaii, wait a week and bring him back? Give her the quote and she'll tell everybody at the Rotary meeting that charter is "too damned expensive."

We could probably support the entire existing charter fleet just on the business we should be getting, but aren't.

If we could identify and sell those trips on which charter gives the customer a profit, rather than a cost, we could change the entire industry.

We've all seen hardworking companies use charter once, then again, then more and more often as they learn to spot the problems that charter can solve. Then they make the big step—they begin to plan their work with charter in mind. They put charter in their business toolbox and lo, a real customer, a steady customer, is born to us that day.

(Caution: This works only with hardworking companies. If the boss is a playboy/playgirl to whom charter is merely a new luxury, be careful. This type usually doesn't last long in the marketplace. Fly them, but collect for each trip.)

GA is an even better business tool now that airline fares are climbing. Much of my business is through agents, and lately they're calling to ask how much it would cost me to get the job done "in one of those little airplanes." They've learned that I can sometimes—not always, but sometimes—get to small towns and remote resorts cheaper than the airlines can take other speakers. They haven't yet learned that other speakers could charter GA aircraft, and I'm not gonna tell them. Maybe you should.

Maybe you should put on a seminar and invite the business travel decision makers in your market. Tell them you don't want all their travel business, just the trips where you can save or make money for them. Show them how to combine trips, travel directly to small towns, take the people they need to get the job done on one trip, and cut down on motels, meals, and bar bills.

(Those last three items are biggies and getting bigger. When I first got into business travel, a room was $8 and three meals totaled about the same. Today the room TAX is $10 and breakfast alone requires a small business loan. Forget about a prime rib for dinner.)

The time is ripe. Right now every—and I do mean every—firm that travels is looking for ways to contain travel costs. They're dead serious about it and receptive to new ideas. They'll let you in and they'll listen.

If nothing else, maybe you should just mail this column to your best charter prospect. When he calls for that Hawaii trip, tell him that's a job for the airlines. Then tell him about the kind of trip on which GA shows a profit—doing the job that can't be done any other way.

Ralph's Update:

This is still a good way to sell charter—go after the jobs that can't be done any other way. This column is still correct except that airline fares have dropped relative to charter rates. On the other hand, businesses strive to cut travel costs even more now than then. By the way, I wrote a series of charter sales letters for NATA on this concept, and they still have them for NATA members.

🐦 🐦 🐦 🐦

Discipline, then leave it alone (May 1991)

"Hey, Ralph," some of you ask, "how come you never write about the bad stuff? You write that goody-goody stuff about happy employees, happy bosses, and happy customers, how come you don't write about the problems? What about discipline? How come you don't write about that? Don't those textbook experts you quote know about discipline?"

Yes, they do. But first, an example from my own experience:

Back in the 1970s I tried to sell Piper's ill-fated ag airplane, the Brave. It was an effort markedly devoid of success. (Piper eventually decided we distributor types didn't know how to sell ag aircraft, so they took over the effort themselves. I'll give them credit; they couldn't sell the Brave just as well as we couldn't.)

One day I showed the Brave to an ag operator (who I *thought* was also the airport manager) and his pilots on the Selma, AL, airport. He—typically—didn't want to buy, but as I climbed in to depart, he said, "Give us a few demonstration passes before you leave."

I put on an airshow.

After the performance, I flew back to Montgomery Aviation where I was employed, and where I found a note saying Mr. Hudgens wanted to see me. Mr. Bob Hudgens was, and still is, the president of the company and very much the boss. The big boss.

I breezed into Mr. Hudgens' office. "You wanted to see me?" "Yes," he said, "I did. Have you ever heard of a fellow named William R. Lockridge?" "Nossir, I don't think so." "Well," he said, "William R. Lockridge is the brand new manager of the Selma airport. He called me about your little airshow, and I spent 15 minutes kissing his ass. Now you call him back and finish the job."

I did. Mr. Hudgens never mentioned the episode again.

Now, what do the textbook experts say about discipline? They say discipline should occur as soon after the deed as possible and in private. Criticism should be of the deed, not of the person. Corrective action should be required and clearly explained. Once the criticism and the corrective action have been completed, the deed should not be brought up again unless it is repeated.

I don't know if Mr. Hudgens ever read the textbooks, but he followed the directions to the letter.

Mother used to say that God is the perfect disciplinarian. Stay in the sun long, you'll get sunburned. Get drunk, you'll have a hangover. Overeat, you'll get a bellyache. Touch a hot stove, you'll get burned. In each case the punishment quickly follows the deed. There's no criticism of the person and no further harping on the deed unless repeated, at which time punishment is inflicted again.

If we could always remember to discipline as per Mr. Hudgens, the texts, and God, we could produce better families, businesses, children, and employees. But, Lord, it's hard to do when you're mad.

What about the good employee who just goofs up? You don't want to run him off or discourage him, but you do want to explain very clearly that backing the fuel truck into a G-IV is not taken lightly.

The texts say leave off the criticism but include the other steps. React promptly. Require action. Then don't harp on it.

For example, after every accident, regardless of the severity, ask the employee(s) involved to provide a written explanation immediately. The report should answer clearly the old questions, who, what, when, where, and why, plus an additional question: How can we prevent this type of accident in the future?

The key words here are immediate and written. Writing a report is difficult and serious and thus better stresses the importance of the event. It must be immediate, because most of us, given 24 hours to dwell on it, can figure out a thousand ways to prove the accident wasn't our fault.

The technique works. I know. I learned it from my first employer, Procter & Gamble, after I wrecked a company car. I sweated over the written report like a mule in July, and I never forgot it.

By the way, save the written report (your insurance carrier will thank you when the lawsuit comes).

Ralph's Update:

Years later I spoke for an aviation group in Florida. William R. Lockridge met my flight, and we laughed about my "airshow." If anyone knows the whereabouts of Lockridge today, I wish they'd tell me how to get in touch with him. I'd like to touch base with him.

🖭 🖭 🖭 🖭

Death of a salesman (Jun 1991)

Willy Loman is dead. Long may he so remain.

Willy, the salesman in Arthur Miller's great drama, "Death of a Salesman," was from the old school. Armed with a "smile and a shoeshine," Willy went forth daily to charm the customer, beguile the customer, sway the customer, sell the customer. His sales kit included great gobs of "hail fellow well met," and very little of anything else.

It didn't work then. It doesn't work now.

Also dead is the concept that great salespeople are charming rogues, quick to tell a dirty joke, break an innocent heart, or twist the truth just a bit in order to close the sale.

Today, the emphasis is on service, dependability, and reliability. Good salespeople don't close sales, they open business relationships. They don't sell and move on, they sell and stay to service. High integrity works better than high pressure, and this is progress.

I didn't dream all this up myself. I stole it from *Forbes, Fortune, Business Week, Inc.*, and other sources. They don't think it up either, but merely report the truths of today's marketplace.

We hear about the customer service revolution from all quarters. It's true, and the best customer service starts with ethical salespeople sincerely trying to help the customer. Nobody can provide good customer service on a product sold by misrepresentation.

When Willy Loman reigned, salespeople were a breed apart. They lived in the "territory" (as per "The Music Man," another great drama about the lovable but shady salesperson), far removed from those people who made, delivered, and serviced the product. Willy didn't even know those people, nor they him. He considered himself better than they, just as they considered themselves better than he.

Today's salesperson can't live that way. She must know, cooperate with, and work with those who produce and service the product. She depends on these people to keep the customer satisfied, just as they depend on her to sell their output.

The quick-closing, hard-pushing, silver-tongued, checked-suited, cigar-smoking hustler is out. The hardworking, long-lasting, trustworthy, steady server of the customer is in.

This doesn't mean we can't all benefit from a little old-fashioned sales effort. The customer can't be served 'til the customer is sold, and that's not likely to change anytime soon.

My shirts come from the laundry starched, folded, and wrapped in a paper band imprinted with these words: "Look better—try our professional dry cleaning." My dry-cleaned suits bear a tag saying "Look better—try our professional laundry service."

The laundry says a lot with those few words. First, they're selling the benefits of their product rather than the product itself. They don't say have a cleaner shirt or suit, they say "Look better." That's smart.

Second, they're cross-selling. If you use their laundry, they sell the benefits of their dry cleaning and vice-versa.

During one busy week in March, I parked overnight and bought avgas at six FBOs in six states. I'm happy to report the service, overall, was excellent. FBOs do provide better service than any other means of transportation, and that's wonderful.

On the other hand, not a single one of the six FBOs tried to sell us anything other than the fuel and parking we requested on our own. Nobody tried to sell us a flashlight, oil change, minor maintenance, sunglasses, maps, wash job, aviation book, altimeter clock, batteries, or sic sacs, even though all of these items were available at one or more of our stops.

Cross-selling makes sense. Divide your annual fixed costs by the number of customers you serve, and you'll find it costs a healthy chunk to get a customer on your ramp. As long as he's there, why not at least offer additional services? If the airplane is in for maintenance, does the customer need charter service during the downtime? Can the aircraft be washed or the interior rejuvenated? Can the avionics be repaired or replaced? There's no end to the opportunities if your various departments just help each other a little.

Ralph's Update:

All of the above is even more true today than in 1991, if for no other reason than the unbelievable spread of the computer. The buyer has more information ever before, and that's going to get more so rather than less so. Sleazy selling just flat won't work; quality selling is more valuable than ever. The good salesperson is now worth top dollar, the sleazy salesperson is near worthless. This is, as Rod Machado might say, a good thing.

⊟ ⊟ ⊟ ⊟

About face! (Nov/Dec 1991)

For years I have preached competition based on customer service, not price.

To quote Hank Williams (that's the REAL Hank, now—Hank, Sr.) I have "saw the light." (Jimmy Swaggart probably said that too, but nobody pays much attention to him anymore).

I am now convinced we must compete on customer service AND price.

At the latest NATA MBA seminar, aviation financial wizard Jeff Susbauer told us that "cost containment" will be the name of the game for successful merchants in the 1990s. "Cost containment." As near as I can tell that's what my mother meant when she said, "Turn out the lights." It's neither high-tech nor glamorous, but it does work.

According to *Business Week,* September 23, 1991, issue, "brand loyalty is eroding as shoppers become more price-minded." Evidently, the public no longer feels name brands are worth the price difference. Dr. Hugh Macaulay, a "Who's Who" economist who tried to teach me something back in the 1960s at Clemson University, sees this from a different angle. He tells me we still buy names we trust, but these names are now often Wal-Mart, Kmart and Sam's. We buy the names of merchants we trust rather than of manufacturers we trust. And we trust those merchants who consistently deliver quality and service at a good price—guaranteed—or your money back.

My latest copy of "Frequent Flyer Magazine" lists several "fine" restaurants around the country that have revamped and changed direction to provide simpler, cheaper menus: menus that provide the biggest bang for the buck.

Southwest Airlines, according to *Forbes* September 16, 1991, works hard at cost containment. It specializes in the quick turn, getting the aircraft back in the air to earn money ASAP. Believe it or not, their cabin and cockpit crews clean the cabin between flights. (Yes, Virginia, that does include pilots.) This at a time when one airline vice president told me the difference between turbine engines and pilots is that the engines quit whining when the trip is over!

Does it work? The front cover of Southwest Airlines' annual report says it all: "In 1990 We Made a Profit." In fact, Southwest made more profit on operations (as opposed to selling assets) than any other major airline in this country last year.

Sam Walton—well, you know about Sam Walton. His proven ability to deliver a sound combination of quality, service, and price—

at a profit—is legendary. *Fortune,* September 23, 1991, tells that story well.

Cost containment and customer service make a powerful pair. Provide the best customer service and the customer will prefer to buy from you at the same price or a little higher. Practice the best cost containment and you'll do better than your competition at any price the market dictates.

And the market does dictate. Make no mistake.

I have a friend who worked his way from nothing to become the owner of five shoe stores, selling fine shoes at fair prices. He looked down his nose at discount shoe stores. Until recently. Recently he closed down two stores, went to New York and bought a bunch of closeouts, discontinued models, and bankrupt stock. He's now in the discount shoe business. That's what the customer wants, he says, so that's what he's going to sell. The market dictated, he responded.

Today's market demands both service and price, and from everything I read, see, and hear, that's going to become more so, not less so. We can moan about the way it oughta be and the way it used to be all we wish. There will still be more fuel brokers, more customers threatening to build their own fuel farms, and more customers just plain haggling over price.

It's one of those horses that gives you little choice. Like it or not, you got to ride or get rode.

Ralph's Update:

In this column I finally got it right about the relationship of quality (service, value) and price. You gotta be good at both. The better you are at quality, the less important price is, but price is always important. If your quality is not there, you will compete on price alone.

1992

"Unforgiven" was best picture. Never saw it, have no idea what it was about. Bill Clinton beat George Bush the Elder in the presidential election, with comic relief provided by Ross "Pie Chart" Perot. The feds passed The Energy Policy Act to "reduce our dependence on imported petroleum." Nobody noticed.

Customers will force you to 'unbundle': (Mar 1992)

Bundling, in olden New England, was a matter of practicality. Winters were cold, heat was expensive, and this made it tough when a young man came calling on a young lady. Believe it or not, it was accepted practice for the young couple to crawl into a bed together—fully clothed, but in bed, nevertheless—while they kept company.

Bundling in aviation is different, but still a matter of practicality. Rather than charge the customer separately for all services provided, the FBO has typically "bundled" all charges together and included them in the price of fuel.

A recent trip pointed out the weakness of the system.

Clyde—my surgeon friend who would rather be a corporate pilot—and I flew in his Mooney to Hangar One, Fulton County Airport, Atlanta. I changed clothes in the men's room; Clyde lounged around their facility for hours in his leather jacket (hoping everyone would think he was a pilot, rather than just a surgeon). We drank their coffee and used their weather machine. The front office person, Rose, couldn't have been nicer if we had topped off a G-IV.

We didn't buy a thing. They didn't charge us a thing.

Is this rare? Maybe, but another sizable operator took a careful count of transient traffic during the last quarter of 1991, and found that 62 percent of the piston-powered transient aircraft, and 30 percent of the turbines, bought nothing. That's nothing at all, as in zilch, nada, nil, nothing, zip.

Folks, there's a problem here. Obviously, the customer is the only person who brings money *into* your FBO. That means those who do buy fuel are paying for services provided to nonbuyers.

The most successful retailers of this decade seem to be those who deliver the best value to the customer—the paying customer—for the buck. How can we do that by charging this good customer enough to pay for services provided to that nonpaying customer?

We can't.

This situation must, and will, change.

It will change not because the FBO wants it changed but because customer demands will force the change.

FBOs in major locations will—must—charge some sort of "facility" or "ramp" fee. (Some of you have already learned not to call this a "service" fee, lest the customer argue that he didn't request service.)

Ultimately, the ramp/facility fee will allow the FBO to provide fuel at a lower price. This will attract those customers who do purchase fuel while driving away those who don't. In the long run, the feeless FBO will attract the nonbuying customers. Since this situation cannot exist for long, that FBO will eventually be forced to charge a fee also.

Cost bundling at FBOs is no longer practical. When courtship bundling became impractical in olden New England, the custom was abandoned. It will happen likewise with FBOs.

Ralph's Update:

Shoot, I just don't know exactly how to rate this one. Seems to me I was partially right and partially wrong. Unbundling did happen to some degree, but nowhere near as widely as I expected. There is less bundling than there was, but it by no means disappeared. Maybe I'll just say the jury is still out on this one.

Message to Congress: *This* is reality (Apr 1992)

Sometimes I speak on the same program with a U.S. Congressperson. Invariably, the group makes a big fuss over the politico and expects me to feel honored at being on the platform with said luminary. I always pretend to be suitably awestricken.

But I'm not.

It's beyond me why a group of successful businesspeople would kowtow to a member of Congress. Why would the head of a profitable business bow and scrape in the presence of one who is, after all, a member of the most miserably unsuccessful group of managers in world history?

Congress has failed horribly by any business standards, yet the individual congressperson is treated like royalty. Why?

Just once I'd like to see a small businessperson stand up and say:

"Congressperson, my little company made a profit last year. In case you don't remember, that means we paid all of our expenses—including the taxes that pay your salary—out of our income and had some left over. Your group, on the other hand, had control over perhaps the biggest budget in the world, and you couldn't live within it.

"Furthermore, my company provided goods and services the customers wanted, priced so low that they couldn't find a better deal anywhere. (If they could have, they would have, since they are free to buy wherever they wish.) Your group, on the other hand, dictated what it would provide at what price and didn't even give us the 'take-it-or-leave-it' option. Still, you delivered lousy goods and services and lost money.

"You inflict and enforce a myriad of incomprehensible safety rules on my business.

"You pass laws dictating what I can and can't do to collect money owed to me. Yet, your collection department—the IRS—uses confiscatory methods to collect on a 'guilty-until-proven-otherwise' basis.

"You tell me I can't discuss prices over coffee with my competitors, but you fix, set, prop up, hold down, and otherwise tamper with prices all over the world.

"You argue with me over the legitimacy of my business expenditures, then you spend part of my money subsidizing tobacco and more of my money on antitobacco programs.

"Congressperson (please excuse me for leaving off the customary 'Honorable' salutation), with all due respect (which isn't much), you might come to our meeting to lecture us on the ways of this nation. Might I not so humbly suggest that we do our jobs one hell of a lot better than you do yours, and further suggest that you should climb down off that ivory tower, sit at our knees, and beg for advice on how you might mend your wicked ways."

I doubt this will ever happen; but, as the song says, "Wouldn't it be wonderful?"

Ralph's Update:

This was probably the most reprinted piece I ever wrote. I got calls from around the company from people who had seen copies in small businesses that had no connection at all to aviation. I enjoyed the notoriety and still believe every word of the column.

No, I don't. But it's still mighty interesting (Aug 1992)

People often ask, "Ralph, do you sell airplanes anymore at all?"

No, I don't.

When I "retired" as sales manager (that's what you call the airplane salesman when there ain't but one airplane salesman) of Huntsville Aviation, it was a clean sweep. I haven't sold an airplane since 1985.

But I have helped a few friends *buy* airplanes.

In June, for example, I helped friend Clyde buy a Baron. (As befits my now-amateur status, I didn't make a dime but do hope to ride in the Baron upon occasion.)

Clyde originally wanted a Cessna 340 but couldn't find one to fit both his budget and his admittedly nit-pickin' standards. He ended up buying perhaps the cleanest 1976 Baron in existence, complete with Colemill conversion and vortex generators.

It was fun, dabbling in the market again. As usual, I learned a few new lessons and relearned a few old lessons.

It is still true that a buyer's inspection performed by an honest technician is worth its weight in street-ready cocaine. (It used to be gold, back when a dollar was still worth 46 cents.)

Page AvJet in Austin did a super buyer's inspection for us twice: once on a 340 Clyde didn't buy and once on the Baron he did buy. Maintenance manager Earl Monreal made the arrangements, and technician Don Martin did the work. Both times, the job was everything a buyer's inspection should be. Don found all the important glitches without running down the airplane. That's worth a lot, and the price of Don's inspection, while not low, was a bargain.

I can't understand why anyone would buy a used airplane without a buyer's inspection. That's like marrying a pregnant woman just to save a little time and effort.

The market today is much changed from back when I could still explain the difference between a flight director and a relief tube. Back in my day, if you had a buyer, you could always find an airplane. Today, it seems, if you find a good airplane you can always find a buyer. Good airplanes are rarer than good buyers.

We used to zip papers around the country via FedEx, and before that, believe it or not, we depended on the mail. Now, everything is done by fax. (Lord help us if the lawyers ever learn that we handle title search, insurance, lien release, financing, and title transfer without their help.)

One thing remains the same: The seller is anxious to "close" the deal during the negotiations, the buyer is anxious to take delivery after the negotiations. Clyde was typical. He rushed out to pick up his new airplane. He rushed to get checked out in it. He rushed to get it home. After all, he wanted to fly it.

After he got it home, he stepped back to admire it, fell off the edge of the Tarmac, and broke his ankle. They say he can fly his airplane in about six weeks, when he gets the cast off.

Ralph's Update:

My role remains pretty much the same, but I have helped friends sell a few airplanes, too. When Clyde got ready to sell the Baron, I helped. Recently I helped another friend sell the airplane I helped him buy more than 15 years ago. He was sick, and smart enough— and ethical enough—to know that his flying days were over.

To meet or not to meet? (Sept/Oct 1992)

Surely by now you know of—and have no doubt taken sides on— the great debate: Should the NBAA trade show take place yearly or every other year?

The publisher of *FBO*, Mike Murrell, says every other year. David Collogan, writing for *Business & Commercial Aviation*, says every year.

I am reminded of Alabama raconteur Shearen Elebash, who once said, "Some of my friends are on one side, and some of my friends are on the other side. As for me, I stand with my friends."

Discretion would surely put me on the every-other-year side, with my publisher and many of my customers. Discretion is not my strong suit.

This debate started when NBAA's Associate Member Advisory Committee—representing the trade show's "big-boy" exhibitors— recommended the trade show be held every other year. Since then, the debate rages on, with various parties arguing this way and that about what the industry "needs." As with most public debates, all participants stress that they argue not for themselves but for the good of the industry.

Uh, excuse me, but whatever happened to the free market system?

Frankly, this is too big a decision to be left to magazine editors, publishers, and writers. What is the correct answer? What is best for the industry? What does the industry need? I don't know, and I don't think any other person or group knows or should be allowed to decide. This is, and should remain, a marketplace decision.

For lo these many years, NBAA has offered to the marketplace a yearly trade show. It has thrived. The exhibitors come to see the consumers who come to see the exhibitors. The marketplace has decided that the industry wants, and is willing to pay for, the NBAA trade show.

Is interest waning? Is the trade show growing less popular? Is demand falling? Does the industry still "need" the trade show?

The marketplace says yes. The 1991 trade show drew record crowds to see a record number of exhibitors in a record number of booths. They—exhibitors and attendees—came voluntarily of their own free will. They looked at the product and decided it was worth the price.

This year? Well, the folks at NBAA speak very carefully these days, but they did admit to me that booth space is already almost sold out. I asked one fellow if booth sales are ahead of last year. He didn't know, but did say, "I don't see how they could be going much better."

Now I ask you, if Coca Cola had a product selling like that, would they be trying to decide if the industry "needs" that product?

NBAA is currently polling members and exhibitors and plans to announce a decision at a press conference at its trade show on September 22. They seek the truth, and I would remind them of the case of Abrams vs. United States (1919), in which it was said, "… the best test of truth is the power of the thought to get itself accepted in the competition of the market." The NBAA trade show has been so tested and found worthy.

Ralph's Update:

One thing befuddles me about this column—where in the world did I run across that quote from a 1919 court case? Damned if I know! NBAA did, of course, keep meeting yearly, and just finished their 2005 convention with record exhibitors even after moving from New Orleans to Orlando in a few frantic weeks after hurricane Katrina smashed into New Orleans.

One big rule fits all (Nov/Dec 1992)

One Big Rule of customer service should be S.O.P. for all employees, from yesterday's new hire to the oldest graybeard on the payroll.

The waitress at our favorite all-you-can-eat buffet restaurant knew the Big Rule, even though she had been on the job only three days.

The fresh fruit wasn't in the line, as it always had been, and we complained—mildly—to our waitress. In less than two minutes the manager arrived at our table bearing a platter filled with a wide variety of fresh fruit. He explained that the fruit was still on the buffet, it had just been moved to a new area and we had missed it. He was sorry we had been inconvenienced and hoped we enjoyed our meal.

We were impressed. Impressed with the manager, of course, for his service above and beyond, but even more impressed that the waitress knew and practiced the Big Rule.

A company in Dallas—named, believe it or not, Mother Dubbers—produces cassette tapes for us and has for years. Recently we forgot to reorder on time and were in danger of running out. We called Mother Dubbers in a panic to see if they could possibly ship a box of tapes within two days. The young lady who took the call didn't think they could work that miracle. We were disappointed but couldn't complain since it was our mistake that caused the problem.

Within ten minutes the owner of Mother Dubbers called us personally. Was there any way, he wanted to know, that he could help solve our problem? We discussed it and he came up with a solution within his means and our needs. It worked.

Yes, we were impressed with the owner's actions. We were even more impressed that the young lady lived by the Big Rule.

The Big Rule is simple: When you can't make the customer delighted—call your boss.

That's it.

Think about it. Isn't that the most important thing you teach your new employee? Wouldn't you feel and sleep better if you knew that every employee lived and followed that one Big Rule? Come to think of it, doesn't your boss want you to follow the same Big Rule?

It's a simple rule, but it takes both teaching and training to make it work. First, you teach it to every employee. That's the easy part. The training, which is harder, comes each time an employee comes to you for help with a less-than-delighted customer.

If your attitude is, "Thanks for bringing this to me. Let's go see if we can satisfy our customer," you will train your employee.

But, your attitude might be, "How come I have to do everything, why did you make him mad in the first place, and why do these jerk customers expect us to be perfect." This, too, will train your employee—but not in the direction you intended.

Ralph's Update:

I didn't dream this idea up, of course, but can take credit for having the good sense to steal it from somebody—I can't remember from whom. It is a great business tool. It is simple, easy to teach, and it works. Hard to beat an idea like that!

1993

"Schindler's List" won best picture. The Mississippi flooded, big time. Son Brett and I took a three-day trip on a Mississippi towboat late in the year and saw where the levees broke. The feds passed the Family Medical Leave Act. The European Union was formed.

Am I the only one left? (Jan/Feb 1993)

Doesn't anyone else believe in the free market anymore? Am I the only one left? I'm talking about real belief, now, not just lip service.

Everywhere I turn, alleged entrepreneurs cry for help. They want the guvmint to alter the marketplace to their benefit.

The airlines want protection in order to "save" our airline industry from foreign competition and foreign investors. We can't make it, they moan, without help. Why don't they quit whining and take a look at Southwest, the airline that has made a profit during each of the last 18 years?

Our farmers want protection, yet we fuss at the Europeans for subsidizing their farmers.

Our automobile industry wants protection.

Ad nauseam.

As near as I can understand the arguments, businesspeople—the same businesspeople who wax eloquent about free enterprise at the Rotary Club—want to protect our country with tariffs.

A tariff, folks, is merely a way to force our citizens to pay more than the going price for foreign goods. It protects a few of our people by forcing all of our people to pay more than the going price on the world market.

The argument is that a tariff on foreign cars, for example, will save jobs in Detroit. And it will. But did you know it costs our citizens more than $250,000 to save a $30,000-a-year job in Detroit? (I've got a Who's Who economist standing by to back me up on that with facts and figures, in case you want to argue.)

To hear our leaders talk (Alabama's Senator Heflin is one of the loudest) you'd think we could seal off our nation and make a living selling to each other. Reminds me of the two farmers who loved the same horse. They sold the horse back and forth to each other for years at progressively higher prices. Then one farmer sold the horse to a man in the next county. "You fool," said the other farmer, "we was making a good living selling that horse to each other!"

Seems to me like the Soviet Union already tested that theory with obvious results.

"But Ralph," you say, "I believe in free trade, but we have to have a level playing field. We can't let their products into America unless they let American products into their country."

'Tain't so. The mere fact that they are willing to punish their citizens with high prices is no reason for us to punish our citizens likewise.

Look at Hong Kong. They have no resources to speak of. They even have to pipe in water, for crying out loud. Yet they thrive, because their citizens are pretty much free to buy and sell on the open market. The world market.

Our country will not thrive on protection *from* the world market, but only by competing fiercely *in* that market.

Ralph's Update:

What worries me is that this column describes the world today just as it fit the world of 1993. As globalization grows, more and more people scream for tariffs. The good news is that we do (mostly) resist them. We are not always successful, but we are trying.

The ITC that used to be (Apr 1993)

Here we go, 'round again, singin' a song about ITC.

I first encountered the ITC (Investment Tax Credit) more than 20 years ago.

In 1972 Piper Aircraft was considering me for a job, and they sent a questionnaire to check my knowledge of general aviation. I didn't get the job (Do you suppose it was the psychological test that did me in?), but I still remember two items on the questionnaire.

Do you think, they asked, that Piper should build a supersonic jet transport? Obviously a trick question. Not, I answered, until they first build and market both a turboprop and a corporate jet.

Then they asked the one I couldn't answer: Do you think the Investment Tax Credit helps sell airplanes? If so, how so?

I had no idea what an Investment Tax Credit was. But even back then I believed it's not too important to know the answer as long as you know somebody who does. I called a top Piper airplane salesman, and he explained the ITC. On the questionnaire I answered the question, then admitted that I had sought help on the answer.

Little did I know how important ITC was to become in my life. It helped me sell literally dozens of airplanes, ranging from crop dusters to corporate aircraft, and my nightly prayers included a special "thank you, Lord" for ITC.

ITC was so important that we sold more airplanes during the last quarter of the year than any other quarter. We sales types were adept at pointing out how a small down payment in late December could create a huge tax break for the year.

To qualify, the airplane had to be used for business. If you couldn't come up with a business use, we could help out with a leaseback.

The airplane had to be "put into service" before the end of the year, and many a new airplane flew a "business" trip on December 31. Fuel was bought and receipts retained for the IRS.

Used airplanes qualified for ITC, but only up to a certain total amount for all used equipment bought by a business during the year. If your customer bought a bunch of used bulldozers during the year, he couldn't get the ITC on a used airplane that year. That put new airplanes at premium, and we milked it like a good cow.

A "new" airplane was one that had never been "put into service." That was a point well stretched by both buyer and seller, and many "experienced" airplanes were advertised as "ITC never taken."

Did we abuse the ITC? Well, let's just say we took full advantage of this opportunity to get back from the guvmint a small part of what they took away. Personally, I felt a strong moral obligation to divert funds away from the guvmint whenever possible. Still do.

The game ended when ITC was dropped in the mid-1980s. Now, they say we're going to get the ITC back. That's to help the businesses they're going to increase taxes on. I don't understand it, but I don't have to. Let the games begin and the good times roll.

One word of caution to airplane salespeople. Back in the old days, many of us, myself included, got so good at selling ITC, leaseback, and fast depreciation that we forgot how to sell airplanes. Don't forget to sell utility, prestige, convenience, and romance. Then show'em how to pay for it with tax savings.

Ralph's Update:

This was one rumor that did not come true. The return of the Investment Tax Credit was not to be—at least so far. But it was fun to remember.

Of dinosaurs and the days ahead (Jun 1993)

Two recent *Fortune* cover stories should be required reading for all businesspeople in general and aviation businesspeople in particular.

To study a sad history of what not to do, read "Dinosaurs?" in *Fortune*'s May 3, 1993, issue.

For a look at the future, read "How We Will Work in the Year 2000" in the May 17, 1993, issue.

These articles are like "Huckleberry Finn" or "Gone With the Wind"—you've got to read them for yourself. They can't be rewritten or summarized, but maybe I can stir your interest so you will read the originals.

"Dinosaurs?" relates the sad but true tales of IBM, Sears, and GM, three firms that once stood high on the mountaintop but have now, as my Southern Baptist friends might put it, fallen from grace. Yes, it could happen to you. You may not be King of the Mountain— even a little mountain—and you certainly aren't as big as Sears, IBM, or GM, but you can fall for the same reasons, nevertheless.

And make no mistake, these three giants have fallen. In 1972, and even as late as 1980, all three rested comfortably among the 20 largest companies worldwide. In 1992 none of them made the list.

Wherein lay the problem, and does it apply to a small business like yours (and mine)? *Fortune* reminds us of the old story of the boiled frog. Putting a live frog into a boiling pot is almost impossible because of the wild fight put up by the frog. Put the same frog into a cold pot, however, heat it slowly, and the frog will sit there calmly and die, fooled by the slow but steady changes in the environment.

(Note: I have never tried this, and don't know if it is true—but it is a great story!)

Fortune suggests the three business dinosaurs sat calmly as the marketplace changed around them, unaware until too late that they were being boiled in their own complacency.

Read "Dinosaurs?" then look at your company, your customers, your competition, and your marketplace. You'll probably find a little bit of the dinosaur attitude in your own situation. I know I did.

Then turn to "How We Will Work In The Year 2000." If you expect to be in business in 2000, this article is a must.

Perhaps the most valuable lesson to be learned from "2000" is that in the future our businesses, our workplaces, and our lives will be driven more and more by the marketplace. Most of you, like I, thought we had been thus driven throughout our lives, but *Fortune* has convinced me that we ain't seen nothing yet.

According to *Fortune*, companies will be smaller, the hierarchical organization will give way to a variety of organizational forms, technicians will become the elite workers, labor will be divided horizontally instead of vertically, we will provide services rather than products, and work itself will be redefined. If all that sounds too complex to grasp, read "2000." *Fortune* explains it far better than I can.

Chances are, you're probably a little curious about all this future stuff anyway. Read these two articles. They're well worth the time.

Then, if you're still curious (or worried), read the April 1993, *INC.* magazine cover story to learn how several companies put it all together to become successful.

Ralph's Update:

The cited articles still make fascinating reading. Did the predictions for business in the year 2000 come true? To a great extent, yes. To some extent, no. Reading the two Fortune *articles in 1993 would have helped you get to the year 2000 and to thrive during the changes. Just as reading the book, "The World Is Flat" will help you understand and adapt to what is happening to the world today.*

Finding a cure for the business blues (Jul 1993)

If you're like me, you've read a zillion theories about the economy. You've learned that the problem is the Democrats, the Republicans, the Japanese, stagflation, deflation, inflation, the Euromarket, the stockmarket, or the meat market.

You know for certain that the solution is quality control, customer service, team building, increased taxation, tax cuts, market expansion, niche marketing, downsizing, and upscaling.

According to *Forbes, Fortune, Inc.* and *National Inquirer*, we're either doomed or on top of the world, and should either get tough or become more kind and gentle if we would survive.

Frankly, I'm confused. If you aren't, please call and straighten me out.

In the midst of all this chaos, I hold these truths to be self-evident:

Nothing will ever return to "normal." Change at an ever-increasing rate is "normal."

The world market is not, and cannot be, controlled by any political party. Neither party caused the changes, neither party can "fix" them. The marketplace is bigger, more complex, and more important than any nation or group of nations, much less any party.

The marketplace works better than any alternative.

Fortunes are made and lost by riding *with* the market, not by bucking it.

You cannot compete on price unless you first master cost containment. Sam Walton beat Sears by lowering his costs, not his profit margins.

The days of the salesman doing it *to* the customer are gone. Likewise, the days when the buyer browbeat the seller. Today, buyers and sellers must work together for mutual survival.

Guvmint is the problem, not the solution. If guvmint makes it more expensive to hire full-time employees, we will become a nation of part-time employees. If guvmint makes it more risky to bring new products to market, there will be fewer new products. Guvmint hasn't learned it yet, but you really can't make the business horse drink, even if you do lead him to regulated waters.

Free enterprise does not exist for business but for the consumer. Any interference with the market costs the consumer. Any time the consumer is not being served by established businesses, new businesses will leap forward to provide that service.

More than anything, I have become fully convinced that success in the foreseeable future will be enjoyed by those companies that cut the costs of sales. Those who fight to maintain price will lose out to those who fight to cut costs, passing the savings to the customer.

These things I do believe. You may disagree, but as for me and my house, we are frantically changing our little business along these lines.

Ralph's Update:

By golly, I stand by this one as is, with no update at all. I hope my grandchildren read this one someday!

Ya gotta have both (Aug 1993)

Good service can't overcome poor product, and good product can't overcome lousy service.

For several years, the North Alabama Lying Pilots Association met every weekday morning at the local International House of Pancakes (IHOP). We met there because of Earline.

Earline is one of the all-time great waitresses. The IHOP itself never was all that hot, but Earline was world class. She babied us, saved "our" table for us, and bought for us (out of her own pocket) a special pitcher because we drank so much water. She was our buddy.

We don't see Earline anymore because we quit going to the IHOP.

Simply put, that particular IHOP was mediocre to start with and got worse. Other IHOPs were nice enough, but ours kept going downhill.

Finally, even Earline couldn't keep us. We left. We went down the street to the Ramada, which has another world-class waitress, Rendy, plus an environment that lives up to the service. We like it fine.

Earline and the IHOP: living proof that even the best service can't overcome a poor product.

Now, to paraphase Paul Harvey, for the other side of the story.

Wife Gail and I always wanted to visit the Virgin Islands. For one thing, the ads showed a paradise like Eden before the snake got in the apple business. For another thing, it sounds so good at a party: "Yes, we're hopping down to the Virgins for the weekend."

Recently, we got our chance. One of our repeat customers actually *paid* me to speak on St. Thomas, and we (big spenders that we are) ponied up for a side trip to St. Johns (the ferry trip is $3.00).

The U.S. Virgins are indeed a paradise. Absolutely gorgeous, and we did it up right. We dined on a veranda while a steel drum band played "Yellow Bird." We drove the back roads of St. Johns. We ate seafood coveted by Neptune, went to beaches where God must swim, and saw scenery that made Lifestyles of the Rich and Famous look, as my mother would say, "just plumb tacky."

It was beautiful.

We will never go back.

Why won't we go back? Because the local natives were a surly lot and quite obviously hated us for being there. The National Park Ranger agreed it was awful, and, like many other people, said, "You just have to get used to it."

But we don't have to get used to it. We can—and did—decide to spend our future tourist dollars elsewhere.

The U.S. Virgins: living proof that even the best product can't overcome poor service.

Service. Product. Ya gotta have both. Either/or ain't good enough.

Ralph's Update:

After this column was printed, the head of tourism for St. Thomas wrote me. He wanted to know two things: 1) Why didn't I contact his department before I wrote the column, and 2) What was the name of the National Park Ranger who said it was awful. My answer to him was also in two parts. I told him that: 1) I had written his department first, and received no response whatsoever, and 2) I wasn't about to tell him who the National Park Ranger was.

By the way—the Northern Alabama Lying Pilots Association rolls on. The Ramada closed years ago and one of our members died recently, but we still meet every weekday morning unless all of us are out of town.

1994

"Forrest Gump" was best picture. To my amazement, one of my most popular funny stories to this day is about Forrest Gump. How much longer can Forrest stay funny? GATT 1994 (General Agreement on Tariffs and Trade 1994) was passed. We're still arguing about it today. An estimated 800,000 Rawandans were killed in 100 days. Some called it warfare. Some called it genocide. O.J. Simpson's wife, Nicole Simpson, was murdered.

You can lead a horse to water... (Apr 1994)

Back in 1993 this column said, "Guvmint hasn't learned it yet, but you really can't make the business horse drink, even if you do lead him to regulated waters."

The following vignettes illustrate the point:

I attended a meeting at which the guvmint explained the new disability laws. The roomful of business owners sat quietly as they were told what they must do for handicapped employees. After the meeting, when the guvmint wasn't listening, they all agreed with the one who voiced his opinion. "I," he said, "am gonna make damned sure we don't hire any more handicapped people. They make good employees, but I don't understand the law, I don't have time to learn it, and I can't afford the liability."

There's a store in Alabama where I have done business—and used the restroom—for ten years. I am no longer allowed to use the restroom. Why? "We can't afford to meet the standards of the new laws, so we just don't have a public restroom anymore." For ten years, I could use their restroom. So could my two handicapped friends. Now, nobody can use it.

Another friend owns a highly regulated business. In the coffee shop one morning, he said, "Well, I've got to figure out who to fire." Why? "The guvmint just passed a regulation that requires a ton of paperwork. It doesn't apply to companies with one less employee than I have. I already meet the requirements of the law, but I can't afford the paperwork. My only option is to fire one employee."

J. T. Townsend, Jr. was a fair-sized electrical contractor in Talladega, AL. He installed the air conditioning in the then-new, now-old Huntsville airport. A few years back, one of his employees left. When someone asked whom he was going to hire as a replacement, Townsend said, "Nobody." Why? "I'm never going to hire another person. The guvmint just makes it too difficult." He never did hire another person and now has no employees at all. If he can't do the job himself, he just doesn't take it on.

(Years ago, in my innocence, I myself hired a person. It was a mistake. It made the guvmint mad. They sent a myriad of forms, rules, and regulations. It was all the fault of my upbringing. We lived in a small town, and Mother and Daddy couldn't be expected to know everything. Hard though it is to imagine today, I actually grew up believing it was a good thing to hire persons. The guvmint taught me otherwise. I explained to my one employee that we could live in sin no more. Unfortunately, she later resumed her wicked ways and became employed again, but at least I wasn't responsible.)

Finally, there is Clyde's story.

Clyde is—make that was—a top surgeon. Other doctors and their families went to Clyde for surgery in his specialty. Clyde just quit being a physician. That's right, he quit! Clyde became a physician, he says, to practice medicine. "The guvmint took all the fun out of it, and they won't let me practice medicine the way it should be practiced, so I quit." Clyde has borrowed a chunk of money to go into another business, hoping to make the money he made as a debt-free physician. "If," he says, "Hillary thinks this is such an overpaid job, she can have it."

All of these people decided they would rather switch than fight. Aren't you glad the guvmint is protecting us?

Ralph's Update:

I still get a little riled reading this column, and I still think the guvmint has caused more unemployment than any other single group. I haven't hired a single person (except for my own wife, Gail) since the 1980s, and probably never will.

Blending roles with complaints (Jun 1994)

John and Martha King, King Schools, gave me the dangdest lesson in handling customer complaints. But before we pass that lesson along, let me tell you what happened to me at the drugstore this morning.

Everybody in our family is allergic to everything from house dust to bureaucrats. We spend a fortune at the drugstore (and they still haven't found anything that works on bureaucrats, but have put house dust in remission by throwing money at it).

Last night, the druggist's assistant goofed on my prescription. I didn't find out 'til they were closed. I was mad. This morning, I called the druggist and let him know exactly how I felt.

The druggist got upset. "Mr. Hood, is there any way we can make up for this? When did it happen? Who was on duty? I'll talk to her about it immediately. Has she ever done this before?"

Frankly, he got so perturbed it worried me a little. "Listen," I said, "I don't want to get anybody in trouble. It really wasn't that important."

"Oh, yes," he said, "it's very important. We can't afford to irritate our fine customers like you. Don't worry, I'll make her aware of the seriousness of the situation."

Well, to tell the truth, I kinda liked that particular assistant, so I spent a few minutes calming him down. It took some selling, but I finally smoothed it over.

Later, it suddenly hit me: The druggist had used the John & Martha King Rule of Handling Irate Customers. The rule goes like this:

When a customer complains to you, there are two roles that will be played out between you and the customer:

1) One of you will try to make a big deal out of the problem;

2) The other person will try to minimize the importance of the problem.

You get to decide which role you will play. The other person will then play the other role.

Isn't that wonderful! And it works.

That's exactly what the druggist did. I started with the "big deal" role. I was mad and making a big fuss about it. But the druggist took that role away from me. He made a big deal of it himself, and danged if I didn't change roles immediately.

He *could* have chosen the "minimize" role. He could have said, "Aw, come on Ralph, it couldn't be all that important." I, of course, would have come right back with, "The hell it ain't important! Let me tell you something …"

Try this idea. Teach it to your co-workers. It really does work.

At least it works for John and Martha King and my druggist.

Ralph's Update:

You just can't possibly imagine how well this idea works until you have tried it yourself. It is truly astounding. Hell, it's even fun!

Can't we all just get along? (Sep/Oct 1994)

As they say down South, y'all ain't gonna believe this!

I *think*—not totally sure yet, but *think*—I'm ready to quit fighting the guvmint and start trying to work with'em. I *think*.

During a recent 13-day period, I drove—as in a car—almost 2,000 miles. (It was one of those schedules you couldn't make on the airlines. It would have been a perfect general aviation trip, except for tropical storm Beryl.)

To make the most of it, I listened to every tape of every presentation given at NATA's April conference in Nashville. Listening to tapes is the most painless way to get an education on dang near any subject. I highly recommend it. (By the way, did I ever mention that *I* have tapes for sale?)

The NATA tapes were wonderful but depressing. Did you ever stop to consider how much of our time we spend just trying to figure out what the guvmint *wants* us to do? Then how much more time we spend trying to do it?

Does the guvmint realize that airports, fuelers, maintenance shops, charter operators, airlines, and other businesses "within the fence" all exit to serve the *customer*, rather than the *guvmint*?

Airports and tenants alike worry about SIDAs (Who's in, who's not?), alcohol and drug testing (When, by whom, and how?), manuals (Is this one "approved" or "accepted"? What's the difference?), environmental issues (How many gallons can we spill before reporting is required? How can we keep the EPA and the local fire marshal happy at the same time?), duty time (Is the guy on duty or on standby, what's the difference and who can tell?), and why in the world did Michael Jackson and Lisa Marie *really* get married?

If there's ever been an area where airports and their tenants are in the same boat, it's guvmint regulation. While we fight over who's responsible for what, we need to remember that we're doing this for the customer, nobody else. We need to divide responsibility and cost so that the customer comes out as well as possible.

But, we must do more. We must try to get the guvmint on our team, so that the airport, tenants, and feds all work together to serve the customer.

I know that sounds impossible, but look at what's happening around us. Management is working with labor (some say that Kelleher's greatest accomplishment is getting unions to work as team members at Southwest), Arabs and Israelis are trying to be nice to one another, and I, for one, have accepted the fact that the Civil War is over. Given those miracles, can't we try, in the words of Rodney King (talk about change—imagine a redneck like me quoting Rodney King) to "get along"?

We must. We simply cannot afford adversarial relationships anymore. Competition won't allow it.

Ralph's Update:

Well, my attempts to get along with the guvmint have been, shall we say, less than totally successful. On the other hand, is it my imagination, or did the guvmint/business relationship improve a bit since the world changed on September 11? Maybe we sort of joined forces against a common enemy. Getting along together got even harder, but perhaps we're all trying a bit harder, too.

1995

"Braveheart" was best picture. It may be best remembered for warriors who—quite literally—showed their asses. The Federal Building bombing took place in Oklahoma City.

Skeptically speaking: watch out (Jan/Feb 1995)

The Republicans are in office. Newt & Company will slash taxes and spending with a terrible swift sword, and all God's chillun gonna get better shoes. Right?

As the song says, it ain't necessarily so.

David Schaffer, counsel, U.S. House Public Works & Transportation Committee (How come it takes such long titles to identify people who work for the guvmint?), pointed out, at a recent learn-to-fly forum in Washington that we can pretty much forget any idea of reduced aviation taxes. Most people don't know diddley about aviation taxes...and care less. To the extent that they think of us at all, they see us as rich doctors in Bonanzas, and they would rather raise than lower aviation taxes. We are not a popular cause. Therefore no politician—Republican or otherwise—can gain points by lowering our taxes.

Many (even some in our industry) say this is as it should be. Aviation is a big recipient of guvmint funds already, and we shouldn't expect more. I can't argue that point; don't want to.

Schaffer warns, however, that we *can* expect to share in the budget-cutting side of Washington's rush to bottom-line thinking. In fact, one of the more popular theories is the "privatization" of the nation's air traffic control system.

I am totally confused about this. Privatization means selling guvmint entities to private owners. England did a lot of that, once they proved to themselves that guvmints make lousy business managers. It worked.

But that's not what they plan for ATC. Instead, they plan to create a "Federal Corporation"—like the Postal Service. If that is privatization, then I'm a brain surgeon.

Can anyone explain to me how changing from one type of guvmint ownership to another will lower costs? Will this work as well as it did for the Postal Service? At that same Washington forum, Phil Boyer, president of AOPA, said we can easily find the answer by asking aviators from countries that have already tried this theory. "They're easy to find," he said, "because they're all in this country taking flying lessons."

If they were going to sell ATC to the highest bidder, I'd probably be for it. UPS, FedEx, and Wal-Mart provide better service than the Postal Service, and I'd give 'em a shot at ATC. This is not a popular attitude.

A few years back, aviation writer Richard Collins wrote that some things are too important to be controlled by the free market. I think some things are too important to be controlled by guvmint. (This is only the second time I've disagreed with Collins in a quarter century of reading his columns.)

Another thing Schaffer said at that forum in Washington: We should all work to get the Aviation Trust Fund "off budget". As long as it's on budget, partially offsetting the deficit, Congress has no incentive to spend it for the purpose for which it was collected. Much as I hate to agree with a Washington lawyer, this guy made sense to me.

Most of us truly believe that the best thing guvmint can do *for* us is to do less *to* us. Schaffer reminded me that we need to keep our guard up—no matter who's in Congress—and work together to that end.

Ralph's Update:

Hoo, boy! Remember when Newt Gingrich and company were at the top of the heap and gonna save us all from guvmint spending and guvmint control? Doesn't seem like it, but that was ten years ago. Guvmint is still talking about "privatizing" ATC, but still can't even agree on what "privatizing" means. As the old saying goes—"The more things change, the more they..."

Bad case of future shock (Apr 1995)

Thirty years ago, when I was a gung ho Procter & Gamble salesman straight out of college, we held a sales meeting in Atlanta. For lunch one day, several of us walked across the street to the bus station. It was a nice place to eat lunch.

Earlier this year, I picked up a package at that very same bus station. It is now a filthy dump. The Hell's Angels wouldn't drink beer there, much less eat lunch.

Could this happen to airports? I hope not, but—like it or not—the elegance is fast disappearing from airline travel.

Back in the 1960s, airline travel had a little class to it. We dealt with the airlines themselves, mostly, and they treated us like they valued our business. Delta would book you on Eastern flights and vice versa. The prices were the same, so you took the most convenient flight. The Atlanta airport had beautiful marble floors and huge columns; men wore ties and women wore gloves.

That was long ago.

Today, only the ignorant deal directly with the airlines. Those in the know avoid the hassle and insultingly poor service: We call travel agents. They answer the phone, get you the best deal, deliver the ticket, provide $100,000 insurance (free), and generally treat you like a human being—all for no additional charge.

That, too, may be about to change. Delta—a once great airline but now one of the hardest to deal with directly—recently capped commissions to travel agents, and other major airlines immediately followed suit. Thus, the travel agent as we know it today may be on the way out.

In the meantime, the majors pull in their horns *and* their service. Regionals fill the gaps but not nearly so comfortably.

What's it all mean? It means that airline travel is more trouble and less pleasant, and it's probably never going to get better.

Airport managers tell me these changes will have no effect on airports. FBO managers tell me this will have no effect on general aviation. Hogwash!

Anything that hurts the airline passenger hurts the airport, and anything that hurts the airport hurts all of aviation as the airport requires additional revenue from general aviation, rental cars, and taxicabs.

My base airport, Huntsville, AL, is a good example. Southwest flies into Nashville and Birmingham, both less than two hours away. Huntsville desperately needs a discount airline, but Southwest doesn't come to towns this size. As we lose business to Birmingham and Nashville, we become even less attractive to the majors, who cut back their services, giving consumers all the more reason to drive to Birmingham and Nashville.

It's a vicious cycle.

I'm part of the problem. As a professional speaker, I *must* keep travel costs down or lose business to competitors who do. So, I often drive to Nashville and Birmingham. Sometimes, I just give up and drive all the way to my destination.

Simply put, airline travel is tougher than it used to be, so I do less of it. Multiply me by a few million, and it's easy to imagine the bus terminal scenario.

This column has no happy ending. I have no solutions.

Ralph's Update:

Everything changed since I wrote this, and I got much of it wrong. The airports became more civilized, not less so, even though they had to adapt to September 11. Yes, airline travel got tougher, but they, too, had to adapt and still are. I don't call travel agents at all these days. I bought my tickets online for awhile through third parties. When those third parties started providing too much frustration, I changed again. Now I research through the third parties and the airline sites, then I call the airlines to buy the tickets. Oddly enough, I seldom pay more than if I book through the sites. I don't understand

that. So—I am back to what I was doing in the 1960s, buying from the
airlines direct.

✓ ✓ ✓ ✓

Risky business: Independents (May 1995)

The guvmint babbles of job creation. In actuality, the guvmint has made the act of employing persons so onerous that everybody is scared to hire anybody. (I, for one, am sworn to never, ever, hire another person. I did it once, and quickly learned that the guvmint doesn't like employers.) We have thus become a nation of part-time employees and/or independent contractors. Home offices abound. (This column is being written by an independent contractor from a home office. For once, I'm on the cutting edge.)

Having made hiring employees undesirable, guvmint is now trying to make it impossible to be an independent contractor, attacking home offices with a knife-in-the-back vengeance matched only by its sabotage of Bob Hoover. As Newt Gingrich said, "At a time when the IRS should be making it easier to have a home office, they make it harder. Now that's foolish—exactly the wrong direction."

Lately it seems to me that every business publication preaches of the horrible risks of trying to get the job done with independent contractors. *Inc.* magazine (September 1994) includes an independent contractor story that could scare an Amway distributor into getting a real job.

I was shocked on a recent Monday when two different people, in separate phone calls from opposite coasts, informed me that many flight schools are changing their CFIs from employees to independent contractors.

Is this a trend? I'm not sure. I've contacted *Flight Training* magazine, NAFI, NATA, AOPA, six large flight schools, and AVEMCO, and I'm still not sure. Everyone seems to agree that the larger, more visible schools are definitely *not* switching from employees to independent contractors. They also agree that many smaller schools have switched, will switch, or are at least considering it.

Everyone, without exception, also agreed that such a switch is risky, and that a mistake could be ruinous—not just expensive, but ruinous. As in losing it all.

Make no mistake about it folks, the IRS *and* various state guvmints are on a rampage when it comes to independent contractors. They don't like them because it's harder to collect from a lot of little companies than from one large company. You cannot simply decide that your CFIs will henceforth be independent contractors, thus relieving you of the problems of workmen's compensation and other reprehensible details brought on by the sin of "employing persons."

If your CFIs are independent contractors, or you are considering moving in that direction, run—don't walk—to your library for a copy of that September 1994 issue of *Inc.* Read it carefully. Study the list of 20—count'em 20—parameters the IRS looks at in order to determine if your independent contractors are actually employees you're trying to pass off as independents.

This is serious business, and the company you save might be your own. As one industry leader put it, most schools simply could not survive the penalties resulting from an adverse ruling in this area.

Be careful.

Ralph's Update:

This is all still true, although I am not certain that the guvmint still attacks with such a vengeance. I do know that many companies in many industries still take a tremendous risk by calling employees—by the guvmint's definition—independent contractors.

Managing under the big top (Jun 1995)

Harvard Business School should go to the circus for a case study. I'm serious.

Recently, I spent an entire day on the circus. Kelly Miller is an old-fashioned tent circus, playing small towns from Texas to Canada, outdoors, under the big top. (You didn't know there were any of those still around, did you?)

I arrived early in the morning. I watched the tent go up, ate in the cookhouse, saw both performances plus the sideshow, and watched the tent come down. Now, more than anything else, I'd love to gather up NASA's rocket engineers and tell them: "Here's a complete circus. Your job is to get it off the trucks and set it up." Lord, I'd love to watch that. I'd bet the farm that the end result would make DIA's construction look well organized!

The circus uses a management system somewhere between utter chaos and lockstep conformity. In little more than two hours, 60-something people arrive in an unbelievable variety of trucks and trailers, unload everything from loudspeakers to elephants, and set up two huge tents plus concessions, a cookhouse, and a wide assortment of rigging, props, wires, and hoses.

Nobody is in charge of everything, but everybody is in charge of something. There is no master plan, but everybody has a job, and everybody does his/her job. *Fast.* You have seldom, if ever, seen people work so fast. They *run* around the lot. Literally.

How, I wondered, do they motivate these people to work that hard? It certainly wasn't money, or a corner office, or a Bigelow on the floor.

Isn't that one of the universal questions of business? How do we motivate the people who actually do the work?

As near as I can tell, the circus does it by creating an environment in which everyone has a stake in the desired goal. For their business, that's simple. In your organization it's more complex, but still doable.

On the circus, the desired goal is to get everything off the trucks and set up—fast—each morning, and back on the trucks—fast—each night. Management's stake in this goal is obvious. What is labor's stake? Simple: As soon as it's set up each morning, labor is through for that morning. They can rest, go to the laundromat, whatever. Likewise, when everything is back on the trucks at night, they're through for the day. Everybody knows this, so they push each other to work fast.

But Ralph, you say, our business doesn't work that way. Well, I said it was more complex, but still doable.

Here's just one example. Next chance you get, visit a Waffle House. As you enter, everyone behind the counter will greet you. That's the desired goal of management. But how do they give labor a stake in the desired goal? At frequent but unannounced times, a mystery shopper—hired by management and unknown to employees—enters the Waffle House. If the mystery shopper is greeted, the greeters receive a reward. There is no punishment if the mystery shopper is not greeted, but a reward if he or she is. Does it work? Like I said, go visit a Waffle House.

Would that work at your business? Try it and see. Set up a simple, clear-cut standard of customer service, then send a mystery shopper around to measure and reward the desired goal. You might be surprised.

Kelly Miller Circus and the Waffle House give workers a stake in the desired goal of management. Try it, it works.

Ralph's Update:

I didn't point out in this column the odd but fascinating fact that my youngest son, Brett, was at the time the ringmaster of the Kelly Miller Circus. (That is explained later in this book.) It was fun to visit Brett on the circus, and I always saw something that I could use in this column (besides, if I got a column out of my visit, I could deduct the trip). I kinda wondered if editor John Infanger would eventually tire of circus columns, but John put me at ease the day he asked, "When are you going to visit Brett again?" "Why," I asked suspiciously. "Because those are the best columns you write."

✓✓✓✓

Huntsville's unique approach (Nov/Dec 1995)

Well, I'll be damned! Our local (Huntsville, AL) airport authority has truly surprised me.

A few months back, this column bemoaned our lack of a discount airline *a la* Southwest or ValuJet. We are two interstate hours from both Nashville (BNA) and Birmingham (BHM)—which do have discount airlines—and many of us make the drive to save airfare.

The more we drive, the less appealing is our airport to carriers, and the harder it is to keep the service we do have, much less attract new service. I saw no solution, and I wasn't alone. Our local newspaper ran a "doom and gloom" article that made my musings appear downright optimistic.

But, hallelujah, our airport authority *did* see a solution, and I am impressed.

Interestingly, their solution started with bad news. They learned that 400 Huntsville area cars were parked at BHM and BNA on a typical day, and that this number was growing rapidly. (Did you know that airports track such info and share it with other airports? I didn't know that.) This was bad news, indeed, but our authority used it to its advantage with a real piece of creative marketing.

As airport marketing director Barbie Peek explains it, they went to our existing carriers—Delta, US Air, Northwest, American—with the bad info and a simple message: "Look airlines, you price Huntsville fares based on the competition, or lack of competition, here in Huntsville. That's a mistake, and it's costing you a bundle. Your real competition is not here, but in BHM and BNA. Look how much business you're losing to those two cities. You need to restructure your fares based on that competition."

Did it work? Each carrier did look and each—without exception—did lower some fares. (Perhaps it should be noted here that our authority had previously earned the respect and cooperation of the carriers by lowering carrier fees rather than raising them when times got tough a few years back.)

And guess what? During September, I spoke in eight states. Not once did I drive to BNA or BHM. And the local paper ran a front-page article bragging about our new, competitive fares.

How much did they lower the fares? Not as much as you might think. You see, they didn't have to get down to BNA/BHM fares. They just had to get down low enough that I was no longer well rewarded for the drive to either city.

By golly, I'm proud of our airport, and appreciative, too. After all, I didn't want to drive to another city in the first place.

****

Change of subject: Congratulations to my aviation *alma mater*, Montgomery (AL) Aviation, on its 50th anniversary in business.

And, thanks to Newark and Atlanta airports for putting pay phones in the area where I wait for the hotel courtesy bus. Curses on all other airports that don't.

Ralph's Update:

I am still impressed by our airport's action. It still works, too. I do drive elsewhere upon occasion, but those occasions are few and far between. Note that at the time, I really wanted payphones on the curb. I still hadn't figured out that cell phones would take over the world.

1996

"The English Patient" was best picture. Alan Greenspan made his famous "irrational exuberance" speech. It was largely ignored until it came true and made him look like a prophetic genius. Clinton beat Bob Dole in the presidential election.

The power of 2 words (Jan/Feb 1996)

It has finally happened.

I have flown airlines for more than three decades. During that time no airline ever apologized for losing my luggage. They searched for it, found it, delivered it, and supplied me with overnight supplies in the meantime, but they never, ever, apologized.

In November, Richard Ellis of ValuJet at Orlando broke the chain. He actually did say the "sorry" word. I was dumbfounded, and remain so. (The bag held tapes that I sell after a speech. Not having the tapes that night cost me at least $100. I was so surprised at the apology that I forgot to get mad.)

Please understand that I don't have a gripe with airline baggage service. Over the years they've lost my luggage infrequently and always did a good job of finding it and getting it to me.

I always wondered, however, why they never apologized. They had, after all, failed to live up to their contract. My life was upset greatly. I would arrive at the airline counter frustrated, worried, and a little panic-stricken, only to be met by a person who obviously considered this a routine, boring situation.

Even if not mad when I got there, I was usually furious after spending *my* time helping them solve the problem *they* caused. (Once, when I pointed out the lack of an apology, the employee said—I swear this is a direct quote—"Well, the apology is written right there on the form.")

Before you shake your head at such cavalier treatment of the customer, ask yourself, "Do *our* employees apologize? Do they know that we *want* them to apologize? Or are they *scared* to apologize?"

I am convinced that, 1) A sincere apology soothes the savage customer beast far better than music; and, 2) The death of the apology is a virtual reality in business today. Nobody apologizes anymore.

Ask for an advertised flavor of frozen custard at your airport. The attendant never says, "I'm sorry, we're out of strawberry." She says, "We're out."

Some managers tell me they don't want their employees to apologize, saying it admits guilt and thus invites lawsuits.

Horse pucky. My friend who owns five convenience stores—he used to be a surgeon, 'til, as he said, the guvmint started telling him how to practice medicine—once filled an 18-wheeler with bad fuel. It ruined the customer's engine. My friend apologized *without* admitting guilt, settled the case cheaply, and kept his customer. He simply told the truth. "We are sorry," he said, "that this happened. We don't want to waste your valuable time arguing about fault, we just want to keep you as a customer. What can we do that will make you happy?"

This works, but it does require that you train and empower your employees. It's trouble, but it's worth it.

****

Under the subject of "The more things change..." An Alabama pilot wrote to Jim Bede for an info packet on his latest "Airplane of the Future." The packet arrived postage due.

Ralph's Update:

This happened more than ten years ago. Not once since then has an airline representative (other than flight crew) told me they were "sorry" about anything. Just recently my bags were delayed overnight. The airline people treated it like a routine matter, which it was to them. To me, it was serious as a heart attack. Pilots and flight attendants, on the other hand, frequently use the "sorry" word about weather, lack of sandwiches, and anywhere else they figure it will help. If they can use that word, how come the airline can't teach it to their other employees?

Getting past a few myths (Mar 1996)

Yessir! We got new airplanes, tort reform, a new attitude, and all God's chillun gonna learn to fly. The money will flow, profits will stick, and flight schools will proliferate like Republicans hunting tax cuts. There'll be a pilot in every pot and the good times will roll. Hogwash.

Dream on, good brethren. Here's the truth: Flight training will not rise up and be counted as a profit center until we learn to treat students like customers—and that's a fact.

Listen to what we keep hearing: Flight training is going to be just like it was in the good ol' days. *What* good ol' days? I don't remember any good ol' days. I don't remember when we ever made a profit on flight training. Do you?

Oh, yes, I do remember when we made money selling airplanes to those on whom we lost money teaching them to fly, but I don't remember when we made money *teaching*.

And, yes, I do remember when we made money (or at least pretended to make money) on guvmint subsidies for flight training, teaching surgeons making $200,000 a year how to become CFIs making $15,000 a year. (Is there anyone left who still pretends that was anything but a huge rip-off of the guvmint?) But I don't remember us making money on flight training.

I totally agree with Bill Monroe, president of Aerospatiale in this country, and about whom you can read more elsewhere in this issue. Bill says we are doomed to failure if we try to recreate flight training as it was: a money-losing proposition.

You really believe new airplanes are going to create excitement, stir the soul, and put a chicken in every hangar? No way. Hell, we had new airplanes for decades, and lost money with them on a regular basis.

Equipment isn't/wasn't our problem. Our problem is attitude. We have never accepted the fact that flight training is a consumer product—an upscale consumer product, at that—and must be marketed as such to people who are then treated like customers, rather than like the bottom chickens on the airport pecking order.

We have a million excuses why we can't sell flight training the way Harley sells motorcycles and Chevy sells Corvettes. Consider just one: "It takes too long to get a license." Yeah? Well, how come we didn't all jump on the recreational license, which at least partially solves that problem? Or, another one: "People can't afford flying." Is that right? Then how can working people buy bass boats and school teachers ski in Aspen?

Perhaps our annual aviation gatherings should put on seminars and workshops from *different* industries this year. Let us hear from those making profits in the motorcycle, sailboat, jet ski, and snowmobile industries. Wouldn't that make more sense than listening to yet another workshop from someone with decades of experience losing money in flight training? Think about it.

We need to create customers, and then we need to treat them in the manner to which our competition has helped them become accustomed. Then, flight training might become profitable, if we do everything else right, too.

Ralph's Update:

I believed all of the above for years before I wrote this, and I still believe it today. But I despair of the industry ever learning it. As a CFI at Moontown Airport, AL, pointed out to me, I have never met anyone who regretted the money spent on flying lessons. Damn, it seems to me that this industry should be able to sell a product like that!

A tech rep's last dance (May 1996)

Jess Krall is retiring.

One of the nicest guys in aviation, Jess has been in the business since about a week after God invented dirt. At least, it seems that way. Actually, about 1960 he went to work with Piper as a mechanic in Lock Haven, and the world of aviation has been more enjoyable ever since.

I met Jess in the mid-1970s. I was working with a Piper distributor and Jess was our Piper tech rep. That's a tough job. The way it worked, if a Piper aircraft was broken, the owner took it to the dealer. If the dealer couldn't fix the problem, the Piper distributor was called in. If the distributor couldn't fix it, the tech rep got involved.

By the time the tech rep entered the picture, it could be a months-old problem with everyone involved—customer, dealer, and distributor—already mad, frustrated, and defensive. The tech rep was expected to come in and solve the problem to everyone's satisfaction.

It was an impossible job. Jess did it well. Jess's primary tools were his own great smile and personality. No matter how bad the day, when Jess arrived you knew things were going to get better.

Looking back, I can't remember that Jess worked any major—or even minor—miracles. What I do remember is the feeling that everything is going to be OK now that Jess is here. He really did care, and he had the confidence of dealer, distributor, Piper, and, within minutes after meeting him, the customer.

Some of you may remember Jess by the nickname, "Dancing Bear." I take full credit for that. He attended our open house one year and I, working the microphone, introduced Jess to hundreds of locals: "I'm sure you don't recognize Mr. Krall in his street clothes, but you have seen him many, many times in your own living rooms. Jess is the original Dancing Bear from the Captain Kangaroo Show." Well, what the heck; nobody had ever *seen* the dancing bear out of costume, so the crowd believed me. Jeff good-naturedly waved to the crowd and a legend was born.

The joke grew. Jess's friends made the most of it, and it was not unheard of for the Holiday Inn marquee to read, "Welcome Jess Krall—Dancing Bear." Jess took it well and, for awhile there, every time he saw me he broke into a silly little dance.

When Jess retired on March 1, he was The New Piper's manager of domestic distribution. You may remember him as the big, jovial fellow who worked the Piper exhibit at big shows like NATA, Sun 'N Fun, Oshkosh, and AOPA's Expo.

The good news is, retired or not, he'll be back this year. Piper let him retire, but they're scared customers will revolt if he doesn't show up at these major events.

Drop by and see him, folks, 'cause, as the circus ringmaster says, "You may never see the likes of this again!" You won't have any trouble spotting him. He looks just like, uh, well, a dancing bear.

Ralph's Update:

No update needed on this one. Everyone who knows Jess will grin when they read it, nobody else will understand it. Jess is still alive, well, and involved in the industry.

The merits of 'small' (Jun 1996)

This is a true story. Names have been changed to protect the author. If this story makes anyone mad, then it's just a lie. I made it up. Everyone knows that half my lies aren't true.

"Tom" had it made. He put in 40 hours per week on his guvmint job and owned a small aircraft maintenance shop on the side. He did the work himself and did it well. Because he had more business than he could handle, Tom was one of the most independent cusses in aviation. You could get an appointment with a brain surgeon quicker than the brain surgeon could get an appointment with Tom.

Once Tom agreed to work on your airplane, it was done his way—period. Mother Teresa would deal drugs sooner than Tom would fudge on an annual. A fellow bought a piece of junk once— one of those airplanes that would lift one wheel at a fire hydrant. He brought it to Tom for an annual. Tom tore it apart, had pieces all over the hangar, and found more problems than Imelda Marcos has shoes. The disgusted owner told him to forget the annual. Just put the plane back together and he'd sell it as is. Tom not only refused, but he told the man that he had 'til Friday to get his piece of ---- airplane out of Tom's hangar. The fellow reconsidered and agreed to do it Tom's way.

Like I said, Tom had it made. Then he retired from his guvmint job. Decided to go big time with his own business. Became the FBO at a larger airport. Borrowed money. Hired people. Was gonna get rich. Went bankrupt instead (and quickly, too).

This was the second time I've seen this scenario. Another fellow went down the same road at the same airport about a decade and a half ago. Did well with a small aviation business part time, then retired from the guvmint and went bankrupt trying to get rich in aviation full time.

In both cases, the same erroneous assumption was made:

If I can make a little money with a little business, I bet I can make a lot of money with a bigger business.

I have seen many people (myself included) prove this to be untrue. Hiring people, buying insurance, keeping records, and other costs/hassles of business have become so high that the law of large numbers—much touted as a business advantage when I was in college—has been reversed in some cases. Today, the small business often has the advantage.

For one thing, the small business doesn't have to toe as many lines as the large company. Right or wrong, like it or not, the little guy just isn't noticed as much as the big boy, and is not regulated as tightly. The same laws don't always apply, and the laws that do apply are not enforced as fanatically.

Management is not spread so thinly in the small company, since managers and managees are often the same people. Employee motivation is less expensive, employee theft less likely, and employee training simpler.

We used to equate growth with success, but it ain't necessarily so any longer. If you are doing well small, you might think twice about your dreams of becoming a megacorp. Downsizing, after all, wasn't invented by the little company trying to get big, but by the big company trying to simplify, to get smaller, to make a profit on less income. AT&T is trying to get more like you. There must be a reason.

Ralph's Update:

I still think the little guy has a lot of advantages. Mostly, though, I think it depends on what you're good at. Some folks are good at small, some at large. Quite often the same folks ain't good at both. I have learned—several times—that small is best for me. I can't think or manage large, and one thing seems to be a truism—it is a big mistake to leave that at which you are good to go into that at which you are not.

Playing the DBE game (Nov/Dec 1996)

I thought affirmative action, quotas, set-asides, and such were on the way out. As the country song sayeth, WRONG! Thanks to the feds, this thinking is alive and well at my local airport and probably at yours.

The Huntsville/Madison County (AL) Jetport, needing to eliminate one rental car company from the terminal for space reasons, put all the spaces up for bids, planning to eliminate the bottom bidder. Budget, which has been there awhile, was next-to-last with a bid of $168,000 per year. Americar, a comparative Johnny-come-lately at our airport, bid $101,000.

Pretty simple decision, huh? I mean, like, you know, with airports needing every dollar they can get, they went for the extra $67,000 and awarded the contract to Budget, right? WRONG!

The contract went to Americar, because it is a DBE, which stands for Disadvantaged Business Enterprise. What is Americar's "disadvantage"? Americar is locally owned by a woman.

Lord, I hate to think of what would happen if I, as a professional humorist, told a joke with a punchline like that. Can't you just hear it? "Well, they were working at a disadvantage—they were owned by a woman." They'd hoot me off the stage in a skinny minute, screaming of political incorrectness with malice aforethought.

In this case, however, it was the feds who labeled woman-owned businesses disadvantaged, and, as we all know, that makes it right. (Incidentally, it would seem logical at this point to wonder if Americar is in any way superior to Budget. I'm the wrong person to ask. I rent cars about 50 times a year, and my travel agent knows that I have for a long time refused to rent from only one company: Americar.)

I asked our airport authority, "How does it serve your customers to turn down the extra $67,000? Or, how does it help the airlines or businesses on the field?" They explained it in clear-cut terms that even I could understand. "Ralph," they said, "the Devil made us do it." No, that's not really what they said. I made that up, but the truth is awfully close to the lie. They explained that the federal guvmint made them do it. Something about 10 percent of the gross revenue from concessions must come from DBEs if you get federal funds for the airport.

"Ah," said I, "now I understand. I guess the feds pay you the $67,000 difference, huh." No, they explained, the feds don't pay any of it. I'm no genius, but it is obvious to me that the airport authority has got to get that missing $67,000 from the other tenants, who have to get it from me and other customers.

Folks, the theory is that the DBE gets the contract because it is owned by a minority. In actual practice, the reverse is often true: The DBE is owned by a minority so it can get the contract. Huntsville, rich in guvmint contracts, teems with businesses set up under minority owners for that very purpose.

How can you compete with this garbage? Well, you can follow the lead of Showalter Flying Service. They sold the FBO to Kim Showalter, who was born in Puerto Rico and is decidedly a woman, just so they could qualify as a DBE and thus play the game on a level playing field.

Hmmm…I wonder if I could get rednecks classified as a minority?

Ralph's Update:

This one made a few folks mad, and some of them still aren't over it. Still, it seems to me that it just had to be written.

1997

"Titanic" was best picture. Princess Diana was killed in a car wreck, giving birth to more rumors than any other death since Elvis died—or didn't die—20 years before. We got Medicare reform this year, but who could tell the difference?

Don't just sell, collect (Mar 1997)

I can't prove it, but I'd bet that collecting—or lack thereof—causes about as many small business failures as any other single problem.

Chisel this in granite: **Collecting is part of the sale.** Procter & Gamble prints on the bottom of its sales forms, "The sale is not consummated until the goods have been paid for." Each salesperson is trained from day one that collecting is, indeed, part of the sale.

Collecting doesn't start *after* the sale; it is *part of* the sale. The selling process and the sales contract, written or oral, must include the terms of collection as well as other details such as price, amount, and delivery.

Sell tough and collecting is easy. Sell wishy washy and collecting is tough. Terms are part of sales negotiation, even part of the sales presentation. Believe it or not, this can actually help the salesperson. When the buyer asks for a concession, the salesperson might pause for a second, then say, "Well, when will we get paid?" You'd be surprised how often buyers will fall over themselves agreeing to pay early, in order to get the concession they want.

Still, there will be collection problems after the sale. The key here is to act early. Nowhere does the squeaky wheel get the grease and the early bird get the worm more certainly than in collecting. The older the debt, the more likely it will never be collected.

One reason we agree on terms is so we can identify problems and act quickly. If they don't pay on time, you've got a problem. That's why so many companies offer discounts like 2 percent 10, net 30, which means, "This is not due for 30 days, but you can deduct 2 percent if you pay in ten days." The company is offering a 2 percent discount if you pay 20 days early, and that's the equivalent of a 36 percent annual percentage rate (simple formula available upon request). When I taught this in college, my students wondered why a company would pay 36 percent just to get paid early. Did they need money that badly? No, but they know any customer in strong financial condition will take that discount. Any customer who doesn't, therefore, bears watching.

As soon as terms are not met, take action. Immediately. What action? Well, a family friend went into business for himself. He didn't know how to collect. He bought something from Rich's (Atlanta's famous department store) and he didn't pay them. Rich's sent him a lot of letters over a period of weeks, with the last letter threatening lawsuit. He then paid the bill, copied the letters, and used them to collect from his own slow customers.

Collect personally. A call from a person who has clout with the customer is more powerful than letters from an unknown person in accounting.

Collect with a reason. Some texts disagree on this, but it works for me. When I'm dunning, I usually give a personal reason why I need the money quickly: It's income tax time; this is our slow season; or, my daughter's college tuition is due. (I'm not going to name names, but a person whose initials are C.J. is going to laugh like hell when reading that one.)

These ideas work when collecting from businesses and individuals. Now, if someone could just tell me how to collect quickly from the guvmint…

Ralph's Update:

Several people asked me if tough collecting makes customers mad. That surprised me. I am convinced that poor collecting causes more ire than tough collecting. Many business people let a customer go without paying for almost forever, then they finally lose their tempers, overdo it and lose the customer forever. Tough, consistent selling and collecting minimize such disasters.

Like a kid—up north (Apr 1997)

This column will not be objective. Wife Gail and I recently spent nine days with the aviation people of Alaska, and the euphoria has not yet worn off.

Any young person seeking a career in aviation should at least consider Alaska. Aviation is different in Alaska; it's more important, more respected, more evident, and more exciting. The whole state—which is more than twice as big as Texas—has about as many people as Birmingham, AL. Half of those live in Anchorage; the rest are scattered all over the place. Seventy percent of the communities, towns, and villages are not accessible in the winter except by dog sled, snowmobile, and/or airplane. The state has more airplanes per capita than anywhere else in this country (and, for all I know, in the world).

This was, in case the IRS is reading, a business trip. I did one workshop, five speeches, and one TV show under the auspices of FAA, the Alaskan Aviation Safety Foundation, and the Northern Alaska Aviation Symposium's Spring Air Fair Expo 1997. We met so many genuine aviation greats that I felt like a pigmy among giants.

A few of our many great experiences...

•   Arriving in Fairbanks close to midnight to find Tom George of the Spring Air Fair Expo 1997 awaiting us at the gate. Talk about hospitality! That was our first indication that Alaskan aviators are a different breed.

•   Our first experience with weather at minus 20 degrees Fahrenheit, plugging up a rental car to a hotel, and seeing the northern lights. Spending a couple of hours with Richard Wien—son of Noel Wien, probably Alaska's most important aviation pioneer—who showed us his photographic history of aviation in Alaska.

• Driving Fairbanks to Anchorage with Tom and Jan Wardleigh on a beautifully clear day during which we saw Mt. McKinley (or Denali, if you prefer the native name), a moose, and more awesome snow-covered scenery than the eye could digest. Flying from Anchorage to Kenai and back with Ginny Hyatt and Tom Wardleigh in Tom's Cessna 180. Tom is a legendary pilot who can and does fly everything from radials to jets. Tom and Ginny are the only two staff members of the Alaskan Aviation Safety Foundation, and they work for $1 a year each. They have to be the best bargain in aviation.

• Flying in Tom Merriman's Super Cub around Kodiak Island. The Cub's tundra tires were higher than my knees, and we touched lightly on a beach. (If that is illegal, I swear it never happened. I make it up. Everybody knows I lie.)

• Learning that cross-country trips require by law emergency equipment, including a gun! Flying in a Cessna 310 with Mike O'Neill, president of Security Aviation, to Homer, where we saw hundreds of bald eagles up close and personal. Being shown around the unbelievably sophisticated aviation department of the University of Alaska—Anchorage, by Bill Butler and Jim Crehan. Meeting and working with the FAA's Ralph Pack and Anne Graham.

• Meeting and visiting with all those wonderful people I spoke for in Fairbanks, Kenai, Kodiak, and Anchorage.

Truth be told, though, what impresses my redneck friends the most is that we ate at the northernmost Denny's in the world—in Fairbanks.

Ralph's Update:

I still remember that trip with wonder in my heart. Tom Wardleigh, one of the true legends of Alaskan aviation, has died since then, as has Mike O'Neill. The bald eagles still congregate at Homer, and I see pictorials of them often. Alaska is a great and wondrous place, particularly for aviators.

Tempt not, lest ye be... (May 1997)

Recently I attended a seminar on how to keep employees from stealing from the company. I learned a lot, most of which can be summarized in five words: accountability with checks and balances.

Decades ago, one of the toughest businesspeople I know—a bottom-line man who owned a string of fast-food outlets—said it very simply, "Show me a manager who fires an employee for stealing and I'll show you a manager who isn't doing her job. Maybe she's not doing her paperwork on time, or maybe she's not checking the register very often, or maybe she's not keeping tight inventory controls. Most people want to be honest, but we owe it to them not to make dishonesty easy."

In other words, to paraphrase The Lord's Prayer, "Lead them not into temptation." And "them," by the way, includes management types.

Back in the 1960s, I had a boss—let's call him Larry—who was quite literally the best in the world at his job. In fact, he was better than anyone else who ever held that job, before or since. Larry grew up in a small-town family of modest means. He moved to the big city, was very successful, made the big bucks, was president of his professional association, and was an officer in his church and country club.

But, it wasn't enough. Larry associated with people who made even more than he did, and keeping up with them eventually caught up with him. He got into a tight, looked around, and discovered how easy it would be to "borrow" a little money from his company. The first time, it worked liked a charm. He "borrowed" the money and paid it back without getting caught. Lord, it was easy. He did it again, and yet again. The amounts "borrowed" grew each time and the fear of being exposed lessened.

Well, it's an old story, and you know the inevitable conclusion. Larry was caught, fired, and disgraced.

In other cases the end was even worse. One well-thought-of businessperson I knew blew his head off with a shotgun rather than face a company audit the next day. Another killed himself in an airplane, and we will never know if it was suicide, or if his mind was so addled by his indictments that he couldn't handle fuel management in a simple airplane.

In each case, and in others that we all know of, one factor was constant: The criminal was a successful manager, temptation was high, and the first crime was appealingly easy. Above all, there was money lying about that was neither immediately needed nor immediately watched. We should not set such a temptation before others and we should avoid such temptation ourselves. Accountability and checks and balances protect us all.

By the way, I do not practice what I preach. In my tiny little business, Wife Gail handles all of the money, both income and outgo, with neither checks nor balances. After attending the seminar, I told her, "For all I know, you could be stealing money and giving it to a boyfriend."

"That's right," she said, "and don't you forget it."

Ralph's Update:

Since this was written I have seen many more examples of managers yielding to the temptation caused by lax accountability standards and practices. It is always a sad story, and quite often could have been avoided by diligent application of simple rules. (By the way, Wife Gail still handles all of the money in our tiny business. Every now and then I open the checkbook and try to make sense of it, but I quickly give up.)

Tough selling 201 (Jul 1997)

A recent column mentioned "tough selling," and several of you asked for more info on the subject.

Tough selling means handling the problems up front. I've never seen a book on it, but every experienced salesperson will know exactly what that means.

The young, inexperienced salesperson is scared to death of problems, so never mentions them, and hopes they don't come up. Then s/he lies awake at night, worrying about those problems. The older, more experienced salesperson tackles problems head on and up front, then sleeps well.

On my very first retail airplane sale, the customer swore that I never mentioned sales tax until we got to the closing. I say I did. Who is right? I'm not sure, but I do know that Stewart Kimmel taught me how to handle that problem. Early in negotiations, Stewart tells the customer in no uncertain terms, "Every price I quote is plus tax."

Stewart sells agricultural airplanes, and ag pilots love to haggle over airplanes in November when their season is over. He tells them up front, "Now this is November, business is bad, and I'm desperate for sales. I'm going to give you a good price, but that price is for right now only. Don't come back hunting the same deal next spring when business is good."

Bob Mathis, president of Atlanta-based Peachtree Planning Corporation, has 51 financial consultants calling on customers. He tells them in no uncertain terms that they will answer not just the questions the customer asks but also the questions the customer should ask.

Back when I was selling Piper airplanes, the Seneca II was our bread and butter airplane. I learned to say very early that, "This is a great airplane, but you shouldn't buy it if you need to carry more than 800 pounds in the cabin, because of weight restrictions."

In each of the above examples, there is a potential problem. The salespeople have learned that life is more pleasant and more profitable if they get the facts out early and clearly.

Oddly enough, tough selling makes the salesperson stronger. In the first place, if I, as salesperson, bring up the tough facts myself, I will handle them much better than if I sit back and wait for the customer to bring them up. If I bring them up, it is obvious that I am being straightforward. If the customer brings them up, there is always the question: Would I have mentioned it if you hadn't caught me?

Nothing will beat out a young, green salesperson who hides from problems quicker than an old, experienced salesperson who brings up the bad stuff early and firmly.

Tough selling is more important now than it was in the past (Willie Loman really *is* dead), and will be even more important in the future. The customer has more information everyday and thus makes wiser decisions. Ethics are in, sleaze is out.

And, as that great business guru James Brown sings, "That's a real good thing."

Ralph's Update:

I was fortunate to work for some people who demanded and supported this kind of selling. To do it, you must have standards for which you are willing to lose a sale every now and then. I remember once—when times were really tough in the airplane sales business—a good customer called to say he was ready to move up to a piston twin. "But," he added, "I am only flying about 60 hours a year. Do you think that's enough flying to stay current in a twin?" I groaned, bit my tongue, and answered, "No, it's not." He didn't buy the twin. My boss had one comment—"Well, that's the only thing you could have told him." And that was that.

The liability shift (Sept/Oct 1997)

1994's General Aviation Revitalization Act limits a manufacturer's liability to 18 years after production of an aircraft. (That's a simplification but will serve our purpose.) The act is a great step forward, and we can take pride in getting it passed (with more than a little help from our friends).

But, as the song goes, "it ain't necessarily so" that the act means all God's aviation chillun gonna have shoes, nor that we will dwell in the house of zero lawsuits forever.

Respected students and scribes of our industry—people like AOPA's John Yodice, *Flying's* Richard Collins and J. Mac McClellan—pointed out long ago that, in many cases, the act won't eliminate liability but merely passes it from manufacturers to other parties.

Our legal system is like a waterbed. Push it down over here, and it will pop up over there. Legal professionals are skilled at finding *someone* to blame for every bad thing that occurs. If we limit their ability to blame the manufacturer, then they will certainly look elsewhere for what they call "deep pockets."

We were warned early and often that commercial owner/operators and maintenance shops will become more popular "targets of opportunity" (that's military talk). More recently, conversations with AOPA's John Yodice and AVEMCO's Jon Harden have convinced me that the private owner/operator—particularly the wealthy private owner/operator—will become a more frequent target.

Let's say Dr. Gotbucks buys a 17-year old airplane, flies it for two years, then sells it to John Familyperson, who wrecks it, killing himself and leaving behind his widow, Ms. Really Nice Familyperson, and their two children, Pitiful and Helpless. They hire a lawyer, Mr. Robert "Hotshot" Grabbitandrun, Esq., who cannot sue the manufacturer of this 19-year old aircraft.

"Obviously," says Lawyer Grabbitandrun, "someone is responsible for this tragedy and must recompense these fine people." After careful research, consisting primarily of a credit report on Dr. Gotbucks, Lawyer Grabbitandrun decides—to his own satisfaction at least—that Dr. Gotbucks (he of the deep pockets) did, intentionally and with malice aforethought, maintain this airplane in a negligent and deleterious fashion before selling it to Mr. Familyperson. Dr. Gotbucks is guilty of being wealthy, if of nothing else, and that's usually enough. After all, you can fool some of the people some of the time, and those are pretty good odds.

This needn't really happen to change our industry, it just has to cause worry. I first started researching this when trying to convince a physician friend—who does, indeed, got bucks (that's ebonics)—that it is safe for him to buy a professionally built kit plane. After I reported my findings, he decided not to buy.

Aircraft salespersons take note: Insurance does exist to cover this risk. AVEMCO already offers such coverage, others will follow, and thus will be handled this particular bulge on the waterbed of litigation. What next?

Ralph's Update:

It all happened, to varying degrees, but one thing has changed dramatically—insurance is harder to come by. That is partially because of all the above, but partially also because profits are not so easily found in the stock market as they were in the 1990s. That means insurance carriers must make a profit on underwriting—

premiums must exceed claims—and that means either lowering risks or raising premiums or both.

1998

Best picture was "Shakespeare in Love." The Nigerian scam letter was in the news. A little company called Google opened its doors in Menlo Park, CA. How in the world did we ever get along without it?

At last, computers (Jan/Feb 1998)

I have been to the mountain top, and I have seen the other side!

Okay, so it's not original. Martin Luther King, Jr., used it in the 1960s, and he borrowed the idea from a fellow by the name of Moses. Still, it's a good line, and it does provide a lead into this column.

First, a review of some glorious history…

In the 1950s, a student pilot generally got the ground school portion of training in a classroom with a roomful of other students and one instructor. By the 1960s, when I got my private certificate (Epps Air Service, Atlanta), you could take the ground school by yourself, with the help of a diabolical machine that combined a projector with a (vinyl) record. The record gave out information interrupted by loud, obnoxious beeps. Every time you heard a beep, you pushed a button to advance the projector. Lord help you if you got record and projector out of sync. The pace was painfully slow; I remember running the 33 1/3 record at 45 rpm. Sounded funny, but it worked.

By the 1970s, while working with a Piper distributor (Montgomery Aviation), I helped introduce a new system which used videotape. (Remember Betamax?)

This was a great improvement, but still a mechanical nightmare.

Recently, at AOPA's EXPO, I saw the latest system. I was, and remain, astonished. (It is truly amazing, by the way, how many important breakthroughs I have first seen at aviation conventions.)

The new system, developed for the Cessna Pilot Centers (Piper is working on its own program), is all on computer and is interactive. The student watches and listens for awhile, then takes a short test, right on the computer. If question is answered correctly, the computer offers congratulations. If answer is incorrect, the computer replays the portion of the program that covers the information in question. Thus the program progresses at the student's own pace; the student is tested at every step; the program moves on only when the student gets it right; and, maybe best of all, the machinery is electronic, rather than mechanical.

Everybody shout hallelujah!

Ground school ain't ever gonna be the same again. Will the CFI be replaced? Of course not. Rather, the CFI's job will be enhanced. Instead of passing out basic info to the unwashed, the CFI will be teaching finer points to students who learn the basics from the computer. I think it's going to be wonderful.

Some folks will fight this—just as they fought the video program in the 1970s—but it will be a short and hopeless battle. This is the future of education as surely as GPS was, just a few years ago, the future of navigation. My advice is, don't waste your time fighting it. Instead, figure out how to profit from it.

I'm a personal trainer myself, and I know the computer will take over a lot of what I do, and do it better. Should I try to compete head on? Not at all. Instead, I'm going to concentrate on those areas of education that I do better than the computer. I suggest you do likewise.

Ralph's Update:

To my great surprise, part of this column—"Everybody shout hallelujah! Ground school ain't ever gonna be the same again"—was oft quoted in flight school ads. To this day you can Google those

words and find them cited in several flight schools ads. John and
Martha King may still be using them. I'm kinda proud of that.

❋❋❋❋

In touch with users (Mar 1998)

I am a frequent customer of airports, and there's something you
might want to know about me.

Your airport can be an architectural miracle. The traffic flow can
be brilliantly designed and perfectly executed. The landscaping can
be done by the contractor who did the Garden of Eden and the decor
done by Michelangelo. Yet I can still have a bad image of your
airport.

My feelings about your airport usually have more to do with
vendors and paper towels than with all of the above.

Atlanta Hartsfield, for example, is a wonderful airport that has
served me well for more than three decades. Yet I currently bear a
grudge against the whole place.

Why? Because I bought a hot dog there last week, and the women
behind the counter obviously did not know the words customer,
service, and smile. They sold me the hot dog, but appeared to resent
the very fact that I was there.

(It's a shame that I am disgruntled anew at Hartsfield. I was just
beginning to get over the way Hartsfield vendors treated me while
they were preparing for the 1996 summer Olympics.)

Paper towels? I don't care how nice your airport is; if it takes two
hands to get paper towels, I don't like the whole place. It just doesn't
make sense to me that I should wash my hands then turn a crank—the
same crank turned by thousands of other hands—to get a paper towel.
(Hartsfield gets very high ratings on paper towels, by the way. So
does my home airport in Huntsville, AL.)

"Gosh," I can almost hear you thinking, "That Hood must be a
real grouch."

Maybe so (and my wife would agree with you), but I am also one
of your best customers and probably more typical than you might
think. After all, most frequent flyers do belong to airline executive
clubs, just so we can escape the rest of your airport.

Here are two suggestions:

1) If you don't utilize focus groups, start immediately. My local airport authority meets regularly with frequent users and asks them that great question made famous by Ed Koch, New York's erstwhile mayor, "How are we doing?" You will be amazed at the answers and at how easily some complaints can be solved.

During one focus group, our airport director said, "Heck, Ralph, if better paper towel dispensers will make you happy, we can solve that." (No, they didn't go out and buy all new dispensers, they just replaced the old ones as they wore out.)

2) Stress to your vendors that common courtesy is a requirement of the lease.

Use mystery shoppers who give out inexpensive rewards for good service. Pick—and publicize—a vendor employee of the month. Give customers a chance to criticize or brag about vendor employees. Do all of this regularly and consistently.

Most of all, never forget that the aviation user—not the airline, the FBO, or the vendor—is the real customer.

Ralph's Update:

This is more important than ever before. Those of us in the industry get used to certain indignities and almost don't notice them anymore. IN-frequent flyers, however, are often horrified. They ask me how I can stand the hassle of traveling on the airlines. Think of that—once or twice a year they are lured to the airport by prices and schedules. That is our chance to convert them. So what happens? They tell me they will never fly again if they can possibly avoid it, and they are serious! (I will be happy to provide names and phone numbers). We can't eliminate all of the hassles, but surely we could do better with vendors, paper towels, and many other irritants.

✳✳✳✳

Faux pas, all over again (Apr 1998)

We could—giving full credit to Yogi Berra—call this story deja vu all over again.

Years ago, Air Force One came to Huntsville (AL) Aviation, preceded by the secret service, which is one more fanatical outfit. They tried to take over the airport, and any of you who ever dealt with them understand exactly what I mean. (We caught one of them chiseling a hole in our hangar roof. Another wanted to seal up our jet fuel truck for several days. We prevailed in both cases.)

Next came cargo aircraft, with a wide variety of equipment including a presidential limousine. Said limo was parked on our ramp, where it was guarded 'round the clock by a suitably serious fellow who looked like he would enjoy roughing up anyone who dared approach.

I, at the time sales manager of Huntsville Aviation (sales manager is what you call the salesman when there ain't but one salesman), was fascinated with the limo. I stood ten feet back—so the guard wouldn't get the wrong idea—and tried to imagine riding in such a vehicle. The guard suddenly stood up and headed my way.

I went into immediate grovel mode, edging away while making apologetic sounds, certain he was about to attack me with secret and lethal techniques of martial art. I couldn't escape.

Somehow he had me cornered. Just as I was about to drop to my knees and whimper, the guard said, "You wanta sit in it?"

I was dumbfounded. We had been put through hell by the secret service. The entire airport had been investigated and surrounded by armed people in helicopters. A supposedly sterile fuel truck had been brought over from the military base. Questions had been asked, badges had been issued, and rules had been set. We were all terrified lest we violate some rule and be shot immediately with dumdum bullets.

All of this, then a bored guard offers to let me sit in the presidential limousine! I'd like to report that I turned him down, but I didn't. He showed me how to open the special latch (it takes two hands), and I sat in the presidential limousine!

Fast forward to 1998…

One recent night, at an FBO that will remain unnamed, I was in the lobby when a limo wheeled up with a VIP. The VIP walked quickly through the lobby, pilots leaped hurriedly to their feet, pilots and VIP boarded a corporate jet, and engines immediately whined. The FBO night man, who didn't know me from Adam's mother-in-law, proudly informed me, "That's Mr. X. He's president of XYZ company. They're going to Y. That other jet is theirs, too. It's leaving in two hours with their CEO, going to Z."

Deja vu all over again. All of the security inherent in owning a corporate jet was wiped out completely by a bored FBO employee.

Was this your airport? I'm not saying here but will send a copy of this column—complete with explanatory letter—to the manager of the guilty FBO.

****

Change of subject: Praise God from whom all blessings flow. The Huntsville airport has installed a pay phone at the curb, out where folks wait for rental cars and shuttles to hotels. I have requested this for years. I have no idea if my requests had anything to do with the action, but I certainly do appreciate it.

Ralph's Update:

This column was pre-September 11 and pre-cell phones. Surely, the security issues would be handled differently today—wouldn't they? I surely hope so. Still, a bored employee trying to play the big shot is a dangerous person. It's hard to believe I made all of that fuss about pay phones in baggage and waiting areas just before we all got cell phones, but I did. Now I can't remember the last time I used a payphone. The current idea is to let us use cell phones on airlines inflight, but I'm agin it.

❋❋❋❋

Benefits at the circus (May 1998)

I still think Harvard should send MBA candidates to the circus. This was reinforced recently after spending two days at the Kelly Miller Circus visiting son Brett who is one of the youngest circus ringmasters in the country. (He still says this is a fling, but we're beginning to wonder. There are lots of benefits to life as a young circus man, including room, board, wardrobe, travel, and young circus women.)

As usual, I had a great time, learned a lot, and came away convinced that the circus can teach us a lot about good business.

Like all businesses, the circus has to find and keep good employees. That means benefits, as well as salary, and Kelly Miller management seems to understand benefits better than many other businesses.

The perfect benefit must be more important to the employee than it costs the company. It should be something that the company can buy cheaper than the individual.

(By the way, many experts say this is one of the reasons for the high cost of health care. Health insurance purchased by an individual is not tax deductible. Health insurance purchased by a company is. Reacting logically to this illogical situation, employers have been purchasing health insurance for employees for more than 50 years. Since the boss paid the fare, employees had no incentive to haggle over the price of health care, and—surprise, surprise—the cost of health care mushroomed.)

Back to the topic...

Circus parents, like the rest of us, want their children to get a good education.

That's hard, when you're on the road from mid-March 'til November. One solution is "home" schooling, but that's tough when the parents are doing two shows a day. It's harder still when parents are immigrants and English is their second language.

Circus management solved the problem. They hired a teacher—a genuine, certificated, qualified teacher. She set up an approved curriculum, and the kids of the circus have their own school. They meet in the cookhouse, the student/teacher ratio is six to one, all of the parents know and have access to the teacher, and the kids may be getting a better education than yours and mine.

I wish you could see those cute little kids running to class of a morning. They carry book bags, just like cute kids everywhere, and they obviously like their school. They have even been known to ask why they can't have school on Saturday and Sunday, as well as Monday through Friday.

It's the perfect employee benefit: It's worth more to the employees than it costs the company. And, Lord, it would do your heart good to see those little kids.

Ralph's Update:

Son Brett is no longer on the circus. He is now a sonar technician on recovery vessels based in places like Florida, Gibraltar, and England. Still, I remain impressed with the business methods of the circus. They move that show every day, seven days a week, doing two shows a day, unloading, setting up, tearing down, and reloading in each town. They have to be organized.

✺✺✺✺

A lack in phone skills (Aug 1998)

Customer service is improving across the board and across the country, except on the telephone. Many otherwise-great companies treat customers horribly on the telephone.

Oddly enough, telephone companies—who certainly should know better—seem to be the worst of the worst.

All of my business is secured by telephone. The phone bill is my second largest business expense each month, exceeded only by travel costs. I have been a loyal AT&T customer for decades. I agreed with that actor (what's his name?) in the AT&T ads—if you've got a good thing going, why switch?

We were happy with AT&T.

Happy, that is, until this past June when Bob Showalter told me about a wonderful new service from AT&T. I called AT&T to check it out. Think about this: I was a happy customer, calling about buying an additional service. The result? I am now furious with AT&T and determined to do as little business with them as possible in the future. It took several extremely frustrating hours to wade through their complex phone system: hours during which decades of good will were wiped out by the "customer service" department.

There is an opportunity here, particularly if you are a small business. Just by following a few simple rules, you can look like a diamond in a slop jar.

First, for God's sake be sure that people can understand the name of your company when the phone is answered. There is a simple test for this. Give your phone number to someone *not* familiar with your company. Tell them to call, listen, and see if they have any idea what they heard when the phone was answered. (Warning: Do not try this test if you have a weak heart or suffer from hypertension.)

When your employees leave a telephone message on a customer's voice mail or machine, say the name and the phone number not once, but *twice*. ("This is Susan, at Amalgamated Aviation, calling about your aviation services. Would you please call me back at 999-123-4567? Let me repeat that name and number...").

I am absolutely amazed how many people leave me a clear, distinct message, then rattle off their name and number faster than an auctioneer trying to get off early.

If you have one of those automatic "choose from the following options" systems, for crying out loud be sure that there is one option that says, in effect, "If all else fails, push '0' to speak to a real live person." I know that sounds basic, but you'd be surprised. Delta Airlines kept me fooled for several calls one day because I didn't have enough sense to realize that "Administrative Offices" was the correct option to get "Consumer Affairs."

How in the world was *I* supposed to know?

Finally, please avoid my personal pet peeve. I call a company, a real person answers, and I ask for a certain department or person. The line clicks, and I sit there, wondering if I have been cut off, or if I am being transferred.

Have your people say something like, "One moment, and I will transfer you." It makes all the difference in the world.

Telephone communications is one area where a little effort can reap huge rewards. Make that little effort.

Ralph's Update:

Amazing! Nothing has changed! I still have the same pet peeves today. If anything, they are worse, not better. When you add in all of the insanity brought to us by cell phones—loud talkers, ringers going off during funerals, etc, ad nauseum—it's a jungle out there. Here again, the small company not tied up in bureaucracy and technology has a chance to look wonderful in comparison.

Of toilets, loopholes (Nov/Dec 1998)

Recently, a high-powered business magazine quoted a heavy-duty economics professor from an industrial-strength university as saying, "All of economics can be summed up in four words: 'People react to incentives.'"

Yes, they do. Now let us add Hood's Corollary: "Bad laws provide strong incentives to find loopholes."

When calculating the results of a new or proposed law, guvmint folks think statically—they assume that nothing will change. They assume, for example, that a new tax, when applied to the current way of doing business, will produce a certain revenue. People, however, operate dynamically. They change the way they do business to avoid the new law.

About 1986 I attended a seminar outlining new tax laws as they pertained to my little business. One thing I learned was that thereafter I could only deduct 80 percent—soon to be dropped to 50 percent— of the cost of meals on the road. The guvmint assumed that would increase revenue by a certain amount. I assumed I was screwed again. Neither I nor the guvmint foresaw the hotel industry's reaction.

Have you noticed that lately more and more hotels include a "free" breakfast in the price of the room? Did you notice that this began just about the same time that the guvmint cut the deductibility of meals on the road? Hmmm... hotel rooms are 100 percent deductible, meals are 50 percent deductible, so meals are included in the price of the room. I wonder if there is a connection there?

A few years back, guvmint got plumb nasty about deducting the cost of taking one's spouse along on a business trip. At just about the same time, meeting-type hotels quit asking how many people would be in the room. Now they ask, "How many keys will you need?" Reckon there's a connection?

Did you know that federal law limits the flow of water through your shower? That's why you can't get rinsed off in the shower anymore. One shower head manufacturer came up with a truly brilliant response. Its shower head has, in large print, the words: **"Caution: Removing the patented flow-restriction valve will allow more than the maximum legal flow of water!"** Then it provides clear directions for removing the patented flow-restriction valve. Can you guess what shower head is in my home? Can you guess where the patented flow-restriction valve is?

The feds also limit the amount of water a toilet can use per flush. It is not your imagination that toilets stop up more than they used to. Simply put, the toilets don't work. There was even a big expose on TV about this. The result? Toilets are hot smuggling items today coming into the U.S. from Canada.

The moral of all this? The next time the pols tell you that a new law will produce certain new results, it ain't necessarily so.

Ralph's Update:

I still have those great shower heads, but—alas and alack—I now have those hated water-limited toilets. I despise them. In fact, of all the irritants provided by the guvmint, I hate those %#@^&)(&ES toilets the most passionately. We keep the plunger under the bathroom sink now, rather than out in the tool shed, just because of those infernal toilets. I pray that I will never meet the jerk who thought up those toilets. I would love to do him great bodily harm with malice aforethought. There's just something about starting the day with a plunger that makes me hate that guy with a palpable, deep-seated, murderous rage.

1999

"American Beauty" was best picture. Bill Clinton is acquitted in his impeachment trial. Y2K scare sends us all into a panic. John Kennedy, Jr.—remembered by many of us as John-John—is killed in an airplane crash.

T-minus too many years (Jan/Feb 1999)

I finally did it! After all these years, I finally saw a Space Shuttle launch.

I live in Huntsville, AL, where we all feel part of the space program. Wernher von Braun's German rocket team did their work here. Much of the designing and building of space vehicles was and is done here—including Unity, the USA part of the space station currently joined with the Russian part. We don't get as much attention here as do the Kennedy Space Center, Houston, and Edwards AFB, but we know in our hearts that building and designing are more important than launching and retrieving, even if Walter Cronkite never understood it.

So, how come I never got to attend a shuttle launching? Well, I got invited several times but, shucks, it meant traveling a long way to see a launch that might not take place. I never felt I could afford the time and money.

Ah, but the December 4 launch was different. I was already in Orlando, a mere hop, skip, and jump from The Cape (that's what we insiders call it), when Bob, Kim, and Jenny Showalter of Showalter Flying Service invited me to watch the launch from the VIP viewing area. (They had invitations through some big shot group Kim belongs to.)

Such a deal. It started when Jenny—blonde, 24 years old, and cute as a bug's ear—picked me up at my motel in her sporty little red car at midnight (the launch was at 3:30 a.m.). It has been awhile since a good-looking young blonde picked me up at a motel at midnight, and I made the most of it. It took me 15 minutes to get into that car, while I held the door open (and interior light on) so the lobby crowd could see Jenny clearly. She, in the meantime, was trying to get me in fast, in case anyone she knew was watching.

Jenny drove me to the staging area for our NASA bus, where I planned to spend another 15 minutes getting out of her car. Unfortunately, Jenny had gotten smart by then. She was out of that car and 15 feet away in five seconds, trying to pretend she didn't know me.

The bus—complete with driver and guide—drove us to The Cape, where we watched from the same viewing area as Secretary of State Madeline Albright.

It was awesome—like the first lap at Indy, Christmas morning, and your first kiss all tied up together. It had everything—lights, action, noise, history, pride, and one tremendous blast.

We had a huge countdown clock, could hear mission control, and could watch the preliminaries on a gigantic TV screen. The tension built horrifically, almost to the screaming point, and then was released in that beautiful, gorgeous burst and thrust of light, speed, acceleration, crackling noise, and gut-pounding vibration. Experience that without feeling a wave of national pride and euphoria, and you're dead, that's all there is to it.

After it was all over, Jenny drove me back to the motel, arriving about 6:00 a.m. I was so sleepy and tired that I forgot to dawdle getting out of the car.

Ralph's Update:

We had a lot of fun with this column. Jenny says pilots from all over teased her about it. Jenny has long since married a disgustingly young and handsome jet jockey and they have a son of their own.

*That makes Bob and Kim Showalter grandparents, so I—having no
grandkids myself yet—am jealous. It's just not fair!*

A failure to keep pace (Mar 1999)

Hoo, boy!

As I write this, it has been proposed by the guvmint that airlines
pay large sums to pax (that's passengers, if you're not an insider) kept
on board more than two hours over and above scheduled flight time.
Good goshamighty. Talk about the pot badmouthing the kettle!

Let me describe a typical—repeat, typical—airline delay.

On a recent Friday, I was scheduled to leave Huntsville, AL, for
Atlanta at 7 a.m. on Delta flight 1712. I prepared to be there on time.
(I fly Delta a lot, and I have an arrangement with them. If I am not on
board when the plane is ready to leave, they have agreed to leave
without me. They live up to their part of the arrangement.) I arose at 5
a.m. and drove to the airport. The airport had prepared with parking,
gates, counters etc. Evidently, Delta counter personnel had prepared
also, as they were on hand to check me in.

Delta gate personnel, pilots, flight attendants, baggage handlers,
and fuelers had likewise prepared, as did the airport and 100 or so
pax. We were all on time and ready to depart at the appointed hour.
Then the pilot called clearance delivery, and all that preparation came
to nought. We were given a one-hour delay because of flow control.

Now folks, anyway you look at it, everybody did their job except
the guvmint. The guvmint said, in effect, "Sorry, folks, we're not
ready for you." And that, I tell you, is a typical airline delay.

Oh, but Ralph, you say, that was because there was too much
traffic, or the weather was too bad, or etc, and so forth and so on.

Folks, all I know is that more than two decades ago the guvmint
deregulated the airlines but kept control of air traffic control. Since
then, the airlines have purchased more airplanes, hired more people,
and otherwise adapted to the growth of the industry. Today, the
airlines carry more people more places for less money with more
safety than ever before.

What has the guvmint done with air traffic control during those two decades? Is it possible that services provided by the guvmint sector to the airline industry have not kept up with services provided by the greedy, for-profit sector? I am convinced the FAA has some truly professional, dedicated, hardworking, people, but ...

People tell me that the world has changed in those two decades—that nobody could have foreseen the huge upheavals that have taken place throughout the world. Well, I can only repeat myself: Delta was ready when we were. The guvmint wasn't.

I wonder who would come out ahead if Delta negotiated this deal with the guvmint: Delta pays for Delta-caused delays, and the guvmint pays for guvmint-caused delays. You reckon the guvmint would agree to that?

Ralph's Update:

We still haven't built a major airport since Denver, and I still feel much the same way. Chicago and Atlanta are in the process of expanding their current airports, and many of us see that is an exercise in absurdity caused by the wants of politicians rather than the needs of airline customers. But, as Tevye and Randy Travis both sang, "on the other hand," we now know that the airlines had not adjusted all that well to the new world either. The difference is that the airlines (mostly) paid for their own mistakes. Airline travelers and taxpayers seem to be paying for the guvmint's mistakes. All that being said, many people have pointed out that the parts of the guvmint that deal with airports and airplanes may well be doing their jobs better than other guvmint groups. I must agree wholeheartedly. I think that is partly because aviation is so immediate and the job so clear-cut. As one technician put it, "It's hard to procrastinate when your job is to help a jumbo jet land." And as a friend's daughter once pointed out, "It's hard to B.S. when you're flying." Besides, I'm biased—I really believe that on both sides of the guvmint/business wall, aviation just attracts a better class of people.

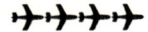

Time for a 1990s tea party (May 1999)

Recently I paid 49.55 percent tax on a car rental at Boston Logan Airport! I swear that's the truth. Taxes and fees totaled 49.55 percent of the rental price of the car. 49.55 percent!

Ten dollars of that was to help pay for a convention center. In other words, they charge visitors $10 to help pay for a convention center to attract visitors. There's something wrong with that way of thinking. (By the way, the car rental lady told me they've been charging that $10 for more than a year and still haven't started building the convention center.)

Forty-nine-point-five-five percent—that is rapacious and confiscatory. It is immoral, indecent, and just plain wrong. Think of it—49.55 percent! And this in Boston, the city that threw tea overboard rather than pay taxes on it.

How do they get the gall to charge such a tax? This is a perfect example of gutless politicians slapping an exorbitant tax on people who don't—can't—vote in said politicians' territory. They couldn't get away with charging their constituents such a tax, so they sock it to travelers.

"But Ralph," people tell me, "every city does that."

Yes, they do. And that's exactly why we've got to do something about it.

Need I remind you that 1) We are in the travel business, and 2) Yes, there is a limit to what people will pay for any product? It really is possible to price an entire industry out of business. If you don't believe that, just ask anyone who remembers trying to sell new airplanes in the late 1970s and early 1980s.

But, what can we do? We certainly can't control local guvmints from coast to coast.

No, but I've got an idea. The federal guvmint is fond of protecting the public from greedy businesspeople, why can't they protect us from greedy local guvmints? Why don't we lobby for limiting the total taxes that can be charged for any product in the country? You reckon we could get a federal law passed stating that total fees and taxes—from all sources—on the sale of any product can never exceed a specified percentage of the product price?

Remember, we did get together and push through changes in product liability laws on aircraft. And that was aviation working alone. On this we should get the help of travel and rental car agents, hotel staff, and others in the travel industry.

I'm serious about this. Something, folks, has got to be done, or where in the world will it end? If it is now 49.55 percent in Boston, where will it go from here? Think of it: 49.55 percent!

Ralph's Updates:

This trend is alive and well. The only defense is to ask for the total price including all taxes and fees up front— then don't read the breakdown of what all is included. Just look at the total. Otherwise, you'll just stay mad! The rental car is still one of the true bargains left in this country. Nothing else provides so much independence for so little money. By the way—you know those signs that warn: "Do Not Enter—Severe Tire Damage Will Result?" They speak the truth and I proved it by totally demolishing four tires in Orlando one day!

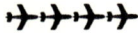

Saturn and beyond (Jul 1999)

Back in the years BS (Before Saturn), buying a car was rated alongside a root canal among those things we most hate to do. A good part of the problem was the haggle factor.

You couldn't get a good deal unless you were a master haggler, and most of us weren't. A Lebanese rug merchant with the knowledge of Buddha might come out okay, but the rest of us suspected we got took. Saturn, with its no-haggle deals, helped change all that.

(It is important to note that the industry changed to suit customers not to suit the guvmint or Ralph Nader.)

In other words, the auto industry is moving from roughneck to genteel. The air travel industry, it seems to me, is moving in the opposite direction.

Back in the 1960s, when I first started riding the airlines, tickets were bought and sold by ladies and gentlemen. Most fares were pretty much the same. You picked the airline that fit your schedule and got a fair deal. Saturday night stays were not required, and you might ride on several different airlines on one trip.

Believe it or not, you could call Delta and end up riding Eastern. If the Delta person found out Eastern had the best schedule, she would book you on Eastern and sell you the ticket herself. Or, she might book you for the first leg on Delta, the second leg on Eastern and the return on United. I swear, young folks, that is true, and it didn't cost a penny extra.

Furthermore, if you were traveling on a $342 ticket to Megalopolis, you could pretty much bet that the person seated next to you didn't pay much more or less.

It really was a no-haggle situation. And fares were based pretty much on mileage, not on the basis of, "If you want to go there, we've got you." (Right now, it costs about $800 to go weekday round-trip from Huntsville, AL, to parts of North Carolina. On the other hand, I just bought a weekday ticket from Huntsville, AL, to Tampa to Gulfport, MS, and back to Huntsville for $311. Go figure.)

Nowadays, there are umpty-ump different fares for the same trip, and no matter what special you bought, chances are the person in the next seat paid less. You really can't get a bargain without a computer and the instincts of Blackbeard the Pirate.

Car rentals are worse. Even if you *do* get a bargain, you can't let up for a second. You have to watch them like a hawk, or they will sell you some special deal. It is a fact that you can buy "discounted" gas deals that will cost $10 a gallon or more for gas used and insurance at an annual rate of over $5,000. The wise get the best deals; the ignorant get took.

Hotels? Don't even ask. It's deja vu all over again.

Now, ask me if I would go back to the genteel days of the 1960s. Not no, but hell no. Today's nitty gritty, haggled prices are a lot lower than yesterday's polite prices. On the other hand, I do believe that the industry—without the help of Nader or the guvmint—will react to customer complaints by becoming a little nicer than a drug pusher in a bad neighborhood. In the meantime, as we say down South, caveat emptor, good buddy.

Ralph's Update:

First, I understand that even Saturn is reconsidering the no-haggle sales technique. The rest of the travel industry certainly hasn't gotten better and may be worse. I used to know all of the answers, now I don't know any. The Economist, one of the most respected magazines in the world, says that between increasing world demand and widespread attempts to cut airlines costs, the airlines may be on the edge of a boom. I hope so. If airlines don't figure out some way to make a profit, it's going to become even more of a jungle out there.

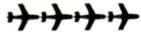

Long on memories (Aug 1999)

The King is dead.

Ed Long, the highest-time pilot in the history of the world, is dead.

Ed was a working pilot who flew more than 50 years for one company, Montgomery (AL) Aviation Corporation. He flew power line patrol in a Super Cub, he loved his job, he had the work ethic of Hercules, and there will never be another like him. He worked long after any ordinary person would have quit, and died of complications of old age.

Ed had more than 64,000 hours, all logged neatly in minutes in a tall stack of logbooks dating back to the 1930s. He averaged well over a 1000 hours a year, year in and year out, for decades on end. I am convinced he enjoyed every minute of it.

Ed was a gentleman and a gentle man. He wore a tie, he was polite to the extreme, and the only time I ever saw him mad was when something kept him from flying. He was a QB and a member of the Alabama Aviation Hall of Fame.

Ed was honest to a fault and the tightest man with a dollar—hell, with a nickel—that I ever knew. He would go to the Piper factory at Lock Haven, PA, pick up a new airplane, bring it back to Alabama, then turn in an expense account for less than $5. (That is not an exaggeration. If you want details, I can supply them, as can many oldtimers at Piper.)

A few years ago, the folks at Moontown Airport in north Alabama invited Ed up for an EAA function. He flew the powerline nine hours on Friday, flew the Super Cub 160 miles to Moontown before 8 Saturday morning, mixed, mingled, and signed autographs, then left before lunch because he had to get back to ferry an Aztec to south Alabama. He was, at the time, 80 years old, and the company had just bought him a brand new airplane to use. I jokingly told everyone he was going to get a vasectomy the following week, and although he feigned embarrassment, I think he rather enjoyed it.

I hope God needs a powerline pilot in heaven, 'cause Ed will drive God crazy otherwise.

****

Total change of subject: In the aftermath of the John Kennedy, Jr. accident, we will probably see a push to ban some combination of VFR, night, single-engine, over-water flight. Let's all do our best to inform the public that such flights are made often, routinely, safely, and productively. Let's remind them that, from a safety standpoint, it probably makes just as much sense to ban night automobile travel. In fact, from a safety standpoint, we should all sell our cars and ride Greyhound.

Ralph's Update:

Ed Long's record may last forever, and his memory will last as long as we who knew him survive. When a few of us get together, somebody will tell an Ed Long story every time. Then we all agree— one more time—that there will never be another like him. I was wrong about the John Kennedy accident. Yes, there were questions, but I saw no big push to limit night flight, and thank goodness. Very possibly that was because our industry did work hard to explain the facts.

2000

"The Gladiator" was best picture. We all woke up on January 1, 2000, in fear and trepidation lest the Y2K bug had removed our world. Nothing happened. Did we overreact to a fear that wasn't there? Or was it preparation that avoided a catastrophe? George Bush the Younger beat Al Gore in much debated presidential election.

Atlanta's answer lies elsewhere (Jan/Feb 2000)

Chicago has two airports served by airlines, New York has several. Houston has two, as does Dallas. Atlanta has one. Atlanta is a mess.

One runway was closed in Atlanta during a few recent weeks. This was preceded by an official announcement that the closure should not cause significant delays. Hogwash.

Atlanta had significant delays before the closure. During the closure it should have been declared a federal disaster area.

My unscientific assessment of the situation comes strictly from my own experiences, which were so miserable that I soon told my travel agent not to book me through Atlanta at all until the runway was reopened.

It's hard to fly out of the South without going through Atlanta, but I did it. I rode commuters, I rode weird routes. But I avoided Atlanta for several trips.

Unfortunately, I had already purchased some tickets through Atlanta that couldn't be changed. Those trips were pure hell.

On one trip to Harrisburg, PA, we were held on the ground in Huntsville, AL, for two solid hours. That, of course, made me miss my connection in Atlanta. No problem, they put me on the next flight. Then they canceled that flight. While running for a third flight, I got into an argument with another man's luggage cart and hurt my foot so badly I was crippled up for weeks. I missed that flight, too. They finally got me on a flight to Washington, DC, where I rented a car and drove to Harrisburg.

Did I mention that they lost my luggage? I stopped at the Big and Fat store and spent $300 on clothes. Couldn't find any size 13 EEE shoes, so made my speech that night in coat, tie, and tennis shoes.

Simply put, Atlanta needs a second airport for airline service. Rumor has it that Southwest once planned to enter the Atlanta market by way of Fulton County airport. Supposedly, the powers that be in Atlanta, gently nudged by Delta, nixed the idea. Also supposedly, Herb Kelleher, Southwest's fire-breathing entrepreneurial leader, retaliated with a vow that Southwest will never serve Atlanta so long as he might live and hold the reins.

Methinks Atlanta screwed up.

There have been many proposals for a second airport in Atlanta, but none that pleased enough people to get the job done. Now, even if they could all agree tomorrow, I doubt they could possibly build one fast enough.

I have a suggestion for Atlanta. Make Dobbins AFB a joint-use airport. It is already there. It is, I am told, underutilized. It is well located. What more could you ask for? Yes, there are political problems, but not nearly so many as in getting Atlanta and surrounding counties to agree on the when, where, how much, and who pays problems of building a new airport from scratch.

Ralph's Update:

In the first place, several people told me that Dobbins is too small and/or landlocked to serve. The recent Southwest crash at Midway in Chicago makes me respect that opinion—besides, I don't know enough to argue the issue. In the meantime, Atlanta has decided to spend a blue kajillian dollars expanding Hartsfield-Jackson airport. I

*shudder to think of it. Ditto with Chicago's O'Hare. I don't know
what the answer is, but damned if I believe more traffic on the ground
and in the air at those two airports is the answer. I will continue to
avoid both of them to the extent possible. Mind you, I am not saying
that both aren't wonderful airports. I just think they are overutilized.*

The midnight rider (Apr 2000)

A little respect, please—I am now an international freight dog. I
spent a recent night in the cockpit of a freight-hauling Atlas Air
Boeing 747-400 (that's the latest version). We took off from
Huntsville, AL, flew to Mexico City and Guadalajara, then returned
to Huntsville, all in nine and a half hours!

I'd like to tell you that I took this all in stride, helped the pilots
handle cockpit duties, and in general remained dignified, but it just
ain't so. Actually, I became a goggle-eyed-kid at first sight of that
giant behemoth of an airplane and remained so throughout the night.

I made astute comments such as shucky dern, golly gee, and
Lawdamighty. It was a right heady experience for a general aviation
pilot more accustomed to ferrying crop dusters than to cruising at
flight level four-one-oh.

Forget every image you ever had of freight hauling in oily twin
Beeches held together by duct tape and safety wire. This was one
more uptown airplane. It was less than two years old and had more
systems than the Pentagon. There were three autopilots arguing
among themselves, three inertial reference navigation systems, and
two GPS systems.

The Atlas Air pilots, Captain John Bloom and First Officer Don
Langford (I just called them Sky God 1 and 2) casually discussed the
relative merits of flying into places like Singapore, Manila, and Kuala
Lumpur (where the heck is that, anyway?). I mentioned my recent trip
to Ames, IA, but they really were not all that impressed.

I had never been in a cockpit larger than a Navajo, and the size of
the 747 was too much for me to truly comprehend. It's like being in
an apartment complex that moves. The nosewheel is ten feet or so
behind the cockpit, so a taxi turn starts long after the crew is hanging

off of the taxiway and over the grass. The crew is some 35 feet above the ground, way ahead of the engines and the rest of the airplane.

On every takeoff, it seemed we rotated way below stall, on every landing we seemed to touch down while still at cruise altitude. I never did get used to it. We did one completely automated approach and landing, all the way to touchdown and roll out. It's enough to give a pilot an inferiority complex.

Atlas Air, Inc., a story in and of itself, is the world's third largest air freight hauler, owns the largest fleet of freight Boeing 747s (including the new 747-400) in the world, operates all over the globe, and is listed on the NYSE, where it has done very well.

On the other hand, Atlas Air owns no ground equipment, hauls no "retail" freight, has no terminals, and no ground crew. Although Atlas operates worldwide, it is paid only in U.S. dollars. Atlas' only customers are major airlines, and basically, Atlas has only one product. It leases B-747s on what is called an AMCI lease—aircraft, maintenance, crew, and insurance are included.

The sales pitch is, "Hey, you've already got the ground crews and equipment and the business, we'll provide the airplane and crew cheaper than you can do it yourself." Talk about niche marketing!

It is no secret that air freight is burgeoning, airlines are concentrating on passengers, and oustsourcing is here to stay. Atlas has positioned itself to run with those trends.

I could write more about my newfound status as a jet-setting freight dog, but I've got to run downtown and get some epaulets for my shirt.

Ralph's Update:

That was one more fun trip! After this was printed, Captain Bill Boehlke, American Airlines, offered to take me in the cockpit on a roundtrip flight to Argentina. Oh, I was excited! Unfortunately, I put it off until I could "get around to it." I was just about ready to get around to it when September 11 came along and changed the world. Captain Boehlke told me flat out, "You blew it, Ralph. No way I can get you on that flight now." Today, even if the world changes back to that nicer, friendlier time, I still won't get to go. Captain Boehlke has retired. I could kick myself!

➡➡➡➡➡

A BBJ Perspective (Jun 2000)

At this year's AS3 Supershow in Tampa, the opening keynoter was Borge Boeskov, president of Boeing Business Jets. Listen, when this fellow drops names, we're talking big-time, industrial-strength names. When he talks about Phil and Jack having a little business lunch, he ain't talking about two good ol' boys down at the local coffee shop—he's talking about Boeing Chair Phil Condit, and GE CEO Jack Welch.

Seems the Boeing Business Jet was born when GE Jack mentioned to Bochair Phil that GE was buying two Boeing 737s for business use, but he wasn't exactly happy with the range. Bochair Phil, who up 'til that point was unaware that GE Jack was making this little purchase of roughly $100 million dollars, said something sort of like, "Well, shoot, GE Jack ol' buddy, I'll see what I can do 'bout that."

Back at the office, Bochair Phil put Borge Boeskov to work on it, and he figured out they could solve GE Jack's little problem by mixing this wing with that fuselage and those engines. Voila, we have the Boeing Business Jet, or BBJ.

Seems the boys from Seattle still didn't know what they had. They told GE Jack they figured they could sell six or eight of the things a year. GE Jack said naw, he reckoned they could sell ten a year. They are actually selling 24 a year.

Near as I can determine, the BBJ runs about 50 million green, then Raytheon finishes them for about another 30 mil or so, and may the good times continue to roll.

Boeskov readily admitted that general aviation is new to him, and his kind of dollar numbers are new to general aviation. At one point he recognized that piston airplane sales are back up, and he thought that was "kind of nice to see." Hell, for many in the industry it wasn't "kind of nice;" it was quite literally a matter of life or death.

Then Boeskov discussed the airline industry, and I, as a frequent-flying road warrior, found myself nodding along with him. His big-picture outlook explained many things that I have noted from my little-picture position.

Boeskov talked of "segmentation" in the airline industry. In the hotel industry, he pointed out, Four Seasons and the Ritz provide luxury at a price; Motel 6 provides low price with no luxuries and damned few necessities.

In the airline industry, a single airline, Delta for example, tries to provide the full range from luxury down through shut-up-and-sit-down economy—all within not only the same company but within the same airplane. Southwest broke that mold danged near 30 years ago, and now we see AirTran et al following suit. Will we also get luxury airlines? That's been oft tried with little success.

All I know is that I am riding Delta less and less and the cheapies more and more, in spite of my Platinum status which gives me free upgrades to first-class on Delta. I just can't justify the difference in the ticket price. If the market totally segments, I know which end I'll be riding.

From a purely selfish standpoint, I hope Boeskov is wrong about airline segmentation. The market seldom heeds my wishes, though, and I fear Boeskov is dead on.

Guess I better get used to the back of the bus.

Ralph's Update:

I am still impressed when I get to hear big-dog speakers like Boeskov. It's one of the great things about conventions. His bit about segmentation has played a big part in the problems of aviation in recent years. Now, let me see if I can explain this so it makes sense: Most "experts" agree that the big problem with the industry has been over supply. Basically, there are more seat miles available than desired at any ticket price that will yield a profit. In the hotel business, the local Marriott that no longer makes a profit can be sold at a distressed price to a hotel chain—Days Inn, for example—that specializes in cheaper rooms. Since Marriott and Days Inn really don't compete, the sale of that hotel effectively reduces the number of high-end rooms on the market. If, on the other hand, Delta sells an airplane, it can end up being sold at distressed prices to another airline that does compete for the same customers at a much lower ticket price. That makes it hard to lower supply.

Hi-tech perspective (Sept 2000)

A few of you might remember me quoting my favorite redneck aviation mechanic, Claudie Drake, in print and in workshops way back in the early 1980s. Well, Claudie is not a redneck mechanic any more. In fact, he's not even Claudie; he is now Claude, or Mr. Drake.

He's not a mechanic, he's Director of Aviation Maintenance (that's what we used to call the shop manager) at Signature Flight Support in Huntsville, AL. You can't even call him a redneck anymore; he wears ties and plays golf, for crying out loud. I can remember when he wore flannel shirts and gigged frogs.

Back when Claudie—er, Claude—was still a redneck mech, he was famous for summing up weighty matters with a few words uttered in full drawl. I walked out into the shop one day and watched for a few minutes as he used an electric screwdriver to unfasten inspection plates on a Navajo. It was the first time I had seen a pro use an electric screwdriver, and I was impressed at the speed. Each screw came out with a short "brrrt...," and Claudie was moving fast.

"Claudie," I said, "that thing saves a lot of time, doesn't it."

"Well," Claudie said, (brrt, brrt, brrt), "it don't save me no time (brrt, brrt, brrt). I'm still working eight hours a day (brrt, brrt). I don't reckon it saves the company no time, cause they're still paying me for eight hours (brrt, brrt). I don't reckon it saves nobody no time except for the customer."

That was about 1979. To this day, I have never heard a better summarization of the benefits of hi-tech. Claudie had it down pat; the business publications are just now catching up.

Remember when hi-tech was gonna produce the paperless office? Remember how it was gonna make us more profits on less work with fewer employees? Remember when it was gonna be a great boon to business? As the Claudie of old might have said, "It ain't happened."

Do you also remember when it was going to cause widespread unemployment? Ain't happened either. Yes, we are all getting more done per hour, day, week, month, and year—but to whose benefit? It seems everything I read these days indicates that the real beneficiary is the consumer.

Yes, we are more productive, but we are also more competitive. Thanks largely to the information age; we now compete with everybody, not just our competitor down the street. The buyer has instant access to the world market and that is gonna get more so instead of less so.

Open up any business publication and you'll find a story about a union that is irate because its industry is outsourcing work overseas. The unions are fighting a losing battle on this. Their companies outsource overseas because their competitors force them to. It's not a choice of outsource or not outsource, it is a choice of outsource or go out of business. That is the way it's supposed to work, and that's the way it will work. If ever there was an unstoppable force, this is it.

Our only recourse is obvious: We need to do those jobs which we do better (more competitively) than anyone else, and outsource those jobs we can get done cheaper elsewhere. Adam Smith explained all of this more than two centuries ago.

The information age does not reduce the price of goods sold. It reduces the costs of making and delivering those goods. That *allows* prices to go down, but competition *forces* prices to go down.

Ralph's Update:

This story is now more than 20 years old, and I have still never heard a better explanation of the benefits of high tech than Claude's screwdriver story. Claude is now, by the way, maintaining a fleet of turboprops and is still a good source of short pithy statements that make big-time good sense.

The meanest regulator (Oct 2000)

Firestone, as Bush the Elder would say, is in deep doodoo. As I write this, Congress, in its infinite wisdom, debates the pros and cons of what to do about Firestone. The Justice Department is trying to decide if it should get into the act.

The usual questions are being asked: Who did what? When? What crime was committed by whom? Who should be punished and how? Is there any way we can blame this on the Republicans/Democrats (pick one)? The mighty ponder, pontificate, and deliberate and will no doubt come up with many weighty decisions sometime in the next few years.

Meanwhile, the meanest regulator in our country has already acted. The meanest regulator has tried, convicted, and meted out severe punishment to Firestone. This meanest regulator wasted no time trying to determine guilt; it acted immediately and cares not a whit about the social consequences of its actions.

The meanest regulator didn't spend one second deciding if Firestone's was a crime of management or owners, or even if there was a crime at all. The meanest regulator didn't like what it saw, and it acted immediately. Punishment was quickly assigned to Firestone's owners. The meanest regulator cares not that some owners had nothing to do with tire production, possible cover-ups, or other actions. Cry though they might of innocence and unknowing, all owners were hit with an unbelievably heavy fine. A fine, in fact, which may well eliminate the once-valuable brand Harvey Firestone created lo those many years ago.

Believe it or not, the meanest regulator, acting with incomplete information and with a brutally casual disregard for the future, fined Firestone's owner, Bridgestone, one billion dollars almost immediately. As G. Gordon Liddy says (when he isn't bragging about his gun and his sexual powers), that is indeed one million million dollars.

The meanest regulator is not some branch of the guvmint. The meanest regulator is the American free market, and that market dropped the value of Bridgestone stock by over a billion dollars in less than six weeks. (That is as of this writing, according to my Merrill Lynch guru, Floyd Taylor).

One billion dollars! And that's just the beginning. They tell me that regardless of what the guvmint does or doesn't do, the Firestone brand may not survive, simply because that same free market may never buy Firestone tires again.

That's tough regulation. You can bet your last dollar that it scared the plu-perfect (as Erskine Caldwell used to say) hell out of all tire makers—indeed all makers of any product. You can bet your Jepp bag they are all saying something along the line of, "For crying out loud, let's make sure that never happens to us!" You can bet they are motivated more by what the market is doing than by what the guvmint might eventually do.

Thus, the public will benefit. And that is, always has been, and always will be the way the market works.

Next time someone tells you that business isn't regulated, tell them about Firestone and our meanest regulator.

Ralph's Updates:

And the beat goes on... Since this was written we have seen Martha Stewart and others hit faster and harder by the market than by the guvmint. Yet people still worry when some industry or another is "not regulated."

2001

"A Beautiful Mind" wins best picture. It really was great. Enron collapses right after I do a speech for them. Wife Gail says they were doing fine until I got there. September 11 changes our lives forever.

Stating the obvious (Jan/Feb 2001)

Well, folks, Bill Clinton has announced the solution to the air traffic problem. Yep, and I am an astronaut, Bush has a mandate, and Jesse Jackson is gonna take a vow of silence. I'm a little sketchy on the details myself, but Dick Branick—an accomplished pilot and a rocket engineer—tells me Clinton's miracle cure involves a new bureaucracy and a watchdog committee. As Dick explained it, the plan doesn't say anything at all about new airports. Humph...

There is, of course, a problem. To paraphrase Churchill, when it comes to airline travel never have so many been so mad at so few. You've seen the reports everywhere from *USA Today* to "60 Minutes." Delays and canceled flights seem more normal than not. Only two of my last ten airline legs have been on the flights I bought tickets for, and that almost seems normal.

But nobody can agree on the problem, much less solve it. One group says it is the airlines' fault for scheduling umpteen flights at the same airport at the same time. Others say it's too few airports and the failure of ATC to improve with the times.

It reminds me of the old question, what do you do when you find yourself at the bottom of a hole? First, you quit digging. The first step for the airline problem seems just as obvious. We should start peak-period pricing ASAP, for all of the reasons stated so well by David Plavin in the last issue of *AIRPORT BUSINESS*. As the young folks say, that is a big "Well, duhhh…!"

But, you wouldn't believe the stink raised by the idea of peak-period. General aviation folks—from the J-3 owner to the G-V pilot—worry that they might be discriminated against. Regional airlines fear likewise. Airports are hesitant to start it because they fear litigation.

Proponents of peak-period pricing say it will help balance the load by luring airlines and pax to currently underutilized airports. Others say pax won't change airports to save a few bucks. Let's kill that argument right now. It does work; Southwest proved it years ago when it chose Midway over O'Hare, Love over DFW, BWI over Dulles, Ft. Lauderdale over Miami, and Providence over Boston. PAX flock to those airports in droves. I'm one of them.

Even that can scare general aviation. If the airlines increase ops at airports that are currently genav airports, where will genav go? We are losing, not gaining, smaller airports, and genav has already been pushed from big-boy airports. (I can remember operating a Cessna Skyhawk in and out of Atlanta's Hartsfield back in the early 1970s. Surely wouldn't want to do that today.)

But the current system can't continue. An unbelievable number of people at the Atlanta airport (I've heard as high as 90 percent) are there just to change planes. They are neither starting nor ending their trip in Atlanta; they're just there for the convenience of the airlines' much beloved hub and spoke system.

As the song says, something's gotta give. For sure, peak-period pricing is no silver bullet. Still, it is the obvious next step. Maybe we could make it more palatable by calling it off-period discounting. Don't laugh; it works for hotels and rental cars.

Ralph's Update:

Well, since then the total resistance to peak-period pricing has diminished somewhat and it is being used to a limited extent. I still like the idea but only if discrimination against genav can be guaranteed in advance. Maybe a four-seat Piper should pay 1/50 the fee paid by a 200-seat transport aircraft. Freight aircraft could be charged by the number of seats that the aircraft could carry. Any other measure—like weight (at gross or with only crew?), speed (at cruise, stall, or approach) or price (retail, fleet, used, new?)—would create too many arguments. Yes, it will be difficult, but, hey, this is important!

Eclipsing reality? (Jun 2001)

I am going to stick my neck out, buck the trend, and risk embarrassment most dire. I hereby state it, out loud and in public: I do not for one second believe the Eclipse jet is ever going to be produced to meet stated specs and price. Admittedly, this comes from the same fellow who predicted the failure of the Lear, the Citation, and the Caravan, but there is a difference.

In those cases, I didn't doubt that they could build the product. I doubted they could sell it. In the case of the Eclipse, it is the other way around; if they can build it they can sell it like mad, but I don't think they can build it.

I have just studied info on the net that insinuates, if it doesn't outright state, that this airplane is a done deal, but it ain't. No airplane really exists until it is certified, produced, and delivered to customers who are happy with it.

Aircraft tend to gain weight and price and lose speed somewhere between the concept and the finished product as delivered to the customer. This has been particularly true of "breakthrough" aircraft.

Am I the only one who remembers standing outside at NBAA in Dallas way back in the 1980s, watching Burt Rutan's scale model of the Beech Starship fly over? Remember all the hoopla on that one? There were some fine aircraft on display at NBAA that year, but the nonexistent, yet-to-be-built Starship stole the show with one flyby and the big announcement. You couldn't talk to people about real airplanes; they were too excited about the Starship.

How about the LearFan? Remember that? How about Jim Bede's promises of aircraft that seemed to defy the laws of physics, all at a price the little people could afford?

Remember the Wing Derringer, the Windecker Eagle, and the Burns? You don't remember the Burns? Hell, I saw the prototype myself, and came away feeling sorry for Cessna, Beech, and Piper because the Burns was obviously going to put them out of business.

Does anybody remember Continental's Tiara engine? Or the Piper Brave that used that engine.

But Ralph, you might well say, some of these products failed simply because they lacked the financing to get to market. The Eclipse doesn't have that problem. No, and neither did the Beech Starship. They threw enough money at that thing to buy OPEC.

Others point out to me the truly substantial people behind the Eclipse, and it is without a doubt a most impressive group. In fact, the people behind it—Harold Poling, Vern Raburn, Dr. Sam Williams, Kent Kresa, Alfred Mann, Chris Finnoff, and Jack Harrington, to name a few—are captains of industry and masters of aviation technology. On the other hand, Bill Lear was solidly behind the LearFan, and he had right impressive credentials himself.

This is another of those times that I honestly and sincerely hope to be proved wrong. I would love to see the Eclipse meet specs and hold the price, but I just don't believe it's possible.

Ralph's Update:

Hoo, boy, did this one ever cause a stir! Some cursed me for being negative. Others often say, well, Ralph, you were right. They couldn't produce it to "meet stated specs and price." No, they didn't. But Lord, y'all, Eclipse did so much more than that. What they did was change the entire face of aviation. They created an entire new spectrum of aircraft being produced by a seemingly endless number of competitors. I still doubt that there will be a jet in every garage or at every charter operation, but by golly, there will be a batch of very light jets out there, and whenever there's that much competition the industry comes out way ahead. My hat's off to Eclipse, and more power to them (no pun intended).

O'Hare and company (Jul 2001)

I write this while cringing in a deep abyss of paralyzing depression. Upon looking up the Chicago *Tribune* website and reading its special report, "Clearing The Air: Solutions to Gridlock," I was horrified. All of my right-wing opinions about the impotency of guvmint bodies were held up, supported, and strengthened by this report.

The *Tribune* has done a masterful job. This is the newspaper, remember, that won a Pulitzer Prize just six months ago for its series on the gridlock at O'Hare. They have, as we say down south, got their stuff together on this subject.

First, they identify the problem as no guvmint bureaucrat would or could. "The airport," says the report, "is and has been a disaster for quite some time." Can anybody argue? (Actually, it could be argued that I have no right to report. I have avoided O'Hare like the plague for years, using it only under extreme duress. I will do almost anything to avoid the place.)

Having thus identified the problem, the *Tribune* outlines a six-step program to solve it. The steps themselves are fewer and simpler than AA's 12-step program, but when the *Trib* went on to explain what must happen for the six steps to become reality, I lost all hope.

The six steps are: More runways at O'Hare; creation of an aviation authority for the area; streamlining air traffic control; reducing overscheduling; a new airport at Peotone, IL (how did any city get a name like Peotone?); and, increasing the use of regional airports.

Simple enough, so what's the problem? Well, the top three are politics, politics, and more politics. All of this requires the cooperation of city, state, and feds amid, and I quote, "the deepening enmity" involved.

Basically, the problem is that the city has O'Hare and no incentive to encourage additional airports. O'Hare wants more runways, but its neighbors don't. The state wants to expand use of other airports while holding up expansion at O'Hare. The city has a Democratic mayor, the state has a Republican governor. As near as I can tell, it's kind of like that line in the old Kingston Trio song, "...and I don't like anybody very much."

Just one example: It takes 18 months to three years to build a new runway, but ten years if you include jumping through all the hoops.

Compare that to the massive highway/bridge destruction caused by the earthquake in California's Bay Area back in 1989. The powers that be let a repair contract to an aggressive businessperson. The contract set a deadline for completion, then set whopping—and I mean really whopping—bonuses for each day the contractor beat the deadline. That contractor had lights up instantly, worked round the clock, finished the repairs in record time, and made great gobs of money.

Here's the Hood plan for the six steps: Sign a contract with Herb Kelleher who is stepping down from the top job at Southwest, and Jack Welch who is doing likewise at General Electric. Sell those two the rights to all aviation in northern Illinois. They'll form a company, sell stock (maybe they will give shares to those who live in O'Hare's traffic pattern), lobby like hell at all levels, and get that job done faster'n Bill Clinton could spot a cute woman at a cocktail party.

Heck, I'd buy some of that stock. Wouldn't you?

Ralph's Update:

I'd tell you exactly how this came out, but I don't know yet. It's still a mess. The Peotone airport was the popular route for a time, then— near as I can tell—"Da Mayor" (Democrat) figured out that would steal taxes from Chicago and political power (the governor is Republican) from him. Now they're planning to spend some multiple of the national debt (okay, so that's a slight exaggeration) on expanding O'Hare. The folks in Gary, IN, say their airport would make a good alternative, and they're trying to lure customers. I hope they make it. In the meantime, Da Mayor bulldozed Meigs Field in the dark of night. And they say we have weird politics down south! Jeesh!

Epps' 38th annual (Aug 2001)

"The 38th Annual..." It has a ring to it, doesn't it? How long has it been—in this up-one-day, down-the-next world we live in—since you've been invited to a "38ᵗʰ Annual" anything? I got such an invitation recently, and therein lies a story.

Way back in 1907, a fellow named Ben Epps built and flew his own airplane. He did a few other things, too, and to this day the municipal airport in Athens, GA, is named Ben Epps field.

Ben Epps had a passel of kids—about nine, I think—and Lord knows the man must have a blue-jillion grandchildren and great-grandchildren. They seem to be everywhere. As best I can tell, all of Ben's children have played a part in aviation. I'm pretty sure that all of the children were pilots, and I know a lot of the grandchildren are.

Members of the Epps clan have owned and operated FBOs, flown for the airlines, led expeditions to retrieve World War II airplanes from the Greenland ice cap, built airplanes, sold airplanes, and owned aircraft. I learned to fly at an Epps operation; I competed with another Epps operation for years; and I had two Epps brothers as customers in other years. I've even been sued with (not by, but with) one of them. Knowing them has been pleasant, enjoyable, and damned interesting.

When I was with Huntsville Aviation, the local newspaper once reported that the airport might oust us from the field in a dispute over lease negotiations. The next day, we were holding a little meeting in the office of Huntsville Aviation's long-time manager, Bill Whatley.

Totally unannounced and without saying a word, George Epps—the Alabama Epps—walked into Bill's office, whipped out a tape measure and proceeded to measure Bill's desk. He did it so busily that he took three different measurements before we got the joke.

Probably the biggest private Fourth of July party in north Alabama is the annual picnic at Sunset Farms, the palatial estate and airstrip of George and Dottie Epps. Every year the Epps Clan gathers there with their many friends for good company and good barbecue. You meet everyone there from astronauts to student pilots, plus a large number of people who only dream of flying. There is a Cub that flies passengers and always at least one antique airplane to ooh and ah over.

This year was different. Little more than a month prior to the Fourth, Dottie Epps died unexpectedly. Dottie was a charming, giving woman, much loved and admired by family and friends. Her death left a huge hole. We all knew there could be no picnic this year. We were all fooled.

Just a very few weeks after Dottie's death, cometh in the mail our invitation to the 38th Annual Fourth of July Celebration Picnic. I was floored. In true Epps style, the family had decided that there could be no greater tribute to Dottie than to hold this and future picnics in memory of Dottie Epps. They did it with class.

There were about 500 people there, including aviation people I hadn't seen in years. They stopped the flyovers briefly as everyone gathered for a short, dignified ceremony in Dottie's memory, then the entire Epps clan joined in to serve barbecue.

I was proud to be there. In fact, I am proud just to know the Epps clan. They are a class act.

Ralph's Update:

In 2005 I attended the Epps 42nd annual Fourth of July Picnic. Interesting. George is remarried to Doris, a longtime friend and business partner. Doris had lost her husband, and she and George later became husband and wife. They are indeed blessed. Also in 2005, Wife Gail and I attended the banquet at which George was inducted into the Alabama Aviation Hall of Fame. I swear the entire Epps Clan was there, and a huge, friendly crowd it was. That was fun.

We shall survive (Oct 2001)

I am reminded of Winston Churchill's statement after Dunkirk: "…we have suffered an ignominious defeat." We have indeed.

As I write this, a few days after events of September 11 changed our world, everyone seems to know what we did wrong and what we should do about it. I do not. My prayer is not that we do what I think should be done but that our leaders have more knowledge and wisdom than I.

That being said, a few comments about our air transportation system…

Some would blame our guvmint and our airlines for "allowing" this to happen. Let us not forget that the goal of our air transportation system is and always has been to allow a free citizenry to travel when and where it wishes, as inexpensively as possible. Our citizenry has demanded cheap, frequent flights. It has not demanded great security and has resisted what security we had. That will change now, and our system will change accordingly. We will trade some convenience for some safety and will probably overdo it for a while.

We will first change those things that will provide the biggest improvement in safety with the smallest investment in dollars, time, and inconvenience. Someone in *USA Today* urged that we put a steel wall—not a door, but a wall—between cockpit and passenger cabin, with a separate outside door for the pilots. Obviously, the writer is unaware of supplemental type certificates, structural criticality, weight and balance, and the time/cost of installing that outside door. No way will we park jets for weeks to install million-dollar doors. I do believe, however, that by the time you read this we will be rapidly installing strong doors between cockpit and cabin, and that said doors will never be opened while passengers are on board. That will provide a maximum safety boost for a minimum investment, and it will happen quickly.

We will give serious consideration to armed guards aboard flights, armed pilots, and other practices currently used by Israel's El Al airline. I think we will also restudy the obvious rewards of joint-use airports, with all of the security thus gained. At all airports security will be upgraded quickly, carry-on baggage will diminish greatly (if it doesn't disappear completely), and passengers will identify checked baggage just as they board (again, as El Al already does it). Travel will be less convenient. We will put up with it.

Reagan National Airport might still be closed when you read this. Indeed, it may never open again. Some say it should have been closed long ago. Airline pilots have told me for years—after a couple of beers and off the record, of course—that they hate the airport for safety reasons, and that was before we started worrying about suicidal airline flights.

Look at a map of the D.C. area. There is no way to protect important targets from airplanes using DCA. If it is kept open, will it be because those in congress are more interested in their own convenience than in safety? (In keeping with the joint-use concept, I wonder if we should put F-16s at Reagan National and let airlines use Andrews AFB?)

Yes, we will survive. The big job is to make sure we survive as
what we are: a free country with (reasonably) convenient travel. I
think we will make it.

As for those who did this, I am again reminded of a Churchillian
quote. Talking on behalf of the English-speaking people following
the attack on Pearl Harbor, he said of the Japanese, "What kind of
people do they think we are?"

Ralph's Update:

*I still get a weird, serious feeling when reading this. I got much of it
right, some of it wrong. We still don't really re-identify our bags just
before boarding, but they will—as I understand it—throw our bags
off if we don't get onboard. Joint-use airports didn't get popular as I
expected. I certainly didn't foresee the emergence of aggressive
passengers or the role they would play. The big question still seems to
be how far can we go toward protecting our citizens before we start
infringing too much on the freedoms and rights of those citizens.*

Feeding frenzy (Nov/Dec 2001)

Wife Gail feeds birds in the back yard. (She also recycles, flosses,
rescues sick animals, gives to the church, and keeps me out of jail,
but this story is about feeding birds.) Gail started by putting up a bird
feeder just for the few birds that were then in our yard. Squirrels ate
some of the bird food, so Gail added a few squirrel feeders. When
chipmunks showed up, she started feeding them, too.

Next thing we knew, we had more birds, more squirrels, and more
chipmunks. The birds were smallish at first until the pigeons arrived.
The pigeons hogged the bird feeders, so Gail asked me to put up
additional feeders designed specifically for little birds. Doves arrived
in large numbers and, being ground feeders, they ate food dropped
from the feeders. Gail started putting special food on the ground for
the doves. She also put up birdhouses for homeless birds. (Gail takes
in all helpless, pitiful creatures. That's how she ended up with me.)

Well, you should see our back yard now. On a typical day, there
are 20 or more pigeons, plus untold numbers of smaller birds mixed

in with chipmunks and squirrels. Walk out our back door and there is a rush and roar as maybe a hundred birds take off at once.

Gail buys food in 50-pound sacks. Every now and then, I ask her how much we spend on birds and rodents. She never knows exactly, but assures me it is, "Not a whole lot." This, from the same woman who can tell you, to the second, exactly how many minutes I talked long distance last month and year-to-date.

In other words, Gail saw a need for a few birds and she filled that need. More came and she expanded the program. She has adjusted for every additional bird and animal. She has met their every need. The result? We have more birds than ever and the end is nowhere in sight.

Across the country, guvmints at all levels are beginning to realize this as a universal problem. Solving needs can and does attract more people with more needs. More welfare begets more people who need welfare. More highways don't solve traffic problems; they just allow more people to participate. (I think they are even beginning to realize—dare I say it? —that California has too many people, rather than too few services).

And—finally getting to the point—bigger airports beget more flights carrying more people. Several recent reports admit that building more runways at already-crowded airports may not (probably will not) solve the problem, but will instead allow those few airports to become even more crowded and more miserable. If you build it, they will indeed come until the misery index is maximized. There really is a maximum number of people that O'Hare can comfortably, safely, and reasonably serve. Ditto Atlanta, DFW et al.

We need more airports in more locations. That will mean both better usage of underutilized existing airports and also the building of new airports. Discount airlines have long since proved that people will willingly fly from alternative airports in major cities. Isn't it time that knowledge becomes a part of public policy?

I would explain this more fully, but I've got to quit now. Gail wants me to put up a specialized feeder for California Condors (Gail fears one might show up any day). Then I've got to drive 100 miles to catch the discount airline at the alternative airport.

Ralph's Update:

Problems attract guvmint money which attracts more people with more problems which attract more... It wears me out thinking about it, and it ain't stopped yet! If anything, it accelerates. What will become of us?

2002

"Chicago" won best picture. It was entertaining, but best picture? Major corporate scandals follow what Enron started. Costs estimated in trillions. Euro introduced in 12 countries.

Selective security (Jul 2002)

Wife Gail and I were returning from a trip to the British Isles. The name of the airline is unimportant. Somewhere over the frozen wilds of Canada, several of the airline toilets quit working. A flight officer left the cockpit, walked to the rear of the airplane with manual in hand and tried to fix the toilet. Am I the only person who thinks there is definitely something wrong with this picture?

We spend billions of dollars on homeland security, great gobs of it aimed at airports and airlines. We passengers have subjected ourselves to untold indignities. Airlines are forced to render cockpit doors difficult, if not impossible, to penetrate. Airports spend like the proverbial drunken sailor. Nothing, it seems, is too much trouble or too expensive if it is done in the name of security. Yet our pilots leave the inner sanctum of the cockpit to repair toilets in flight?

More than that, our pilots leave the cockpit casually to relieve themselves in flight. They also leave that much-vaunted cockpit door wide open while passengers board and depart the airplane.

If I were in charge (and let me be the first to say that only a fool would *put* me in charge) I would prohibit cockpit crews from entering or exiting the cockpit at any time—repeat any time—that passengers are on board. Period.

Wait, I retract that "period." I would also require that the cockpit door be shut and locked when passengers are on board. The only exception would be at such times that the pilots have declared an emergency and determined that said emergency requires one of them to leave the cockpit.

Oh, but Ralph, you ask, how would crews use the "facilities?" Listen, as much money and trouble as we are expending, you're trying to tell me we can't figure out some way to provide the pilot with the proverbial pot to you-know-what in?

Others ask, "But what if a passenger, furious with air rage, goes berserk and is whuppin' up on somebody in the rear cabin?"

Listen, the pilots are responsible for several hundred people and the airplane. They should not leave the cockpit even if—hell, especially if—a passenger in the back is shooting at people. The crew should remain in place and land the airplane ASAP.

Ralph's Update:

Boy I caught a lot of flak on this one, mostly from airline pilots on a web aviation forum. They wanted to know how they were going to…well, you can figure that out. I still say it should be done. They still leave the door open during boarding and deboarding, but they have changed their bathroom procedure. On a more recent long flight, to/from Hawaii, the pilots didn't open the door until flight attendants cleared the area, then rolled a service cart crossways across the aisle between cabin and bathroom. A flight attendant stood behind the service tray, scanning the aisle and looking for all the world like a secret service stalwart on the presidential detail. I was impressed and appreciative.

☆☆☆☆

Ralphonomics 101 (Aug 2002)

What in the world is going on? Terrorism, corporate scandal, stock market drops, and forest fires set by arsons. Will there ever be a "normal" again? I am reminded of Wordsworth's poem of 1807:

"The world is too much with us, late and soon.

Getting and spending, we lay waste our powers."
Ain't it the truth? The news is so bad it takes guts to read a paper or turn on a TV.

I am also reminded of the Kingston Trio's song of the 1960s: "They're Rioting In Africa." Remember the line that went, "The world is festering with unhappy souls"?

Alan Greenspan, in the meantime, looks like a diamond in a slop jar. Five years ago—when we were being told that it was a new era, the old methods of stock evaluation no longer applied, and price-earnings ratios were meaningless—Greenspan warned us of "irrational exuberance." Many laughed at him, and many now wish they had listened.

That was during the era when, as one pundit wrote, investors thought the stock market went up because they were smart. Turned out Greenspan was the smart one. We had forgotten that stocks go up because of profits and not the other way around. Greenspan tried to warn us, but we didn't listen.

That was also during the era when we thought the stock market could and would climb forever. (People thought the same thing in the 1920s—The Roaring '20s—just before the Great Depression changed their minds.)

The scandals of today had roots in that go-go era of the 1990s. Since the stock market was going up, what harm did it do to fudge financial reports a bit, just 'til things got better (which, after all, they always did)? It could all be cleared up with future (paper) profits.

Now we are in trouble and, just like in the 1930s, we are trying to circle the wagons. A few months ago I worried because we were passing steel import tariffs. I wondered if that was a portent of things to come. Now we have passed a 30 percent—repeat, 30 percent—tariff on Canadian lumber. In other words, we have decided to charge all of our citizens 30 percent more than the going market for lumber just so a few of our citizens can charge more for their product. And they call this "fair trade." We, and the rest of the world, did this during the Great Depression; and it both worsened and lengthened the pain.

Another thing: We busily attack pharmaceutical companies because drug prices are high. We think they are making too much profit. But expectation of profit is what drives research. If we cut the expectations, it will cut research and cut the introduction of new drugs. True, nobody will make obscene profits from drugs that are not introduced, nor will the rest of us benefit from those drugs.

Do we in aviation need to worry about all of this? Well, historically, sales of durable goods drop faster than other items in a recession, as do sales of other items that are (like travel) bought with discretionary dollars. Does that describe aviation? Looks like a "duh" to me.

More than anything else in economics, I worry about those two things: increased tariffs (as if we can make a living selling overpriced products to each other), and our tendency to attack profits during scary times. The Soviet Union tried both for more than 70 years. They went bankrupt.

Ralph's Update:

This scares me more now than it did then. Globalization is not just coming, it is here. We must spend our efforts competing in the world market, not trying to protect ourselves from it. I said, "trying" to protect ourselves, because it is widely agreed that we cannot—repeat, cannot—protect ourselves from the world market. Period.

☆☆☆☆

Ethics examination (Sept 2002)

I am concerned. I recently had a conversation with a bright young airline pilot. This fellow worked hard, made all of the right moves and sacrifices, and is now where he always wanted to be—flying a jet for the airlines. It's fun to see a young person reach goals through good, honest efforts, and more power to him. In our latest conversation, however, he shocked me.

I asked how his airline was doing, and he implied that they are making a profit. That didn't agree with what I had been reading, so I expressed my surprise. He then explained that, yes, the company was showing a loss, but that was just because they were "cooking the books." The implication was that this helped them negotiate with the unions.

I asked if he got that information from his pilots' union, and he answered yes.

I asked this young pilot if he honestly believed that the airline could hide large profits from Wall Street analysts. He assured me that he did, indeed, believe exactly that.

Let me say right up front that I do not really believe the union is teaching that; nor do I think the airline is doing that. Let's assume for a moment that the airline wanted to show a large loss where a large profit actually existed. I don't think they could get away with it and don't think they are dumb enough to try it. Nor do I think the union is dumb enough to teach that if it is not true.

No, I do not have faith that the guvmint would catch such efforts. I do have faith in the market catching such shenanigans often enough to make the odds of success too low to warrant the attempt. Yes, I know that Enron and WorldCom did fool some of the people some of the time, but they did get caught, and not by guvmint but by those in the marketplace.

But, forget all of that. The important issue here is not what is true, but what is believed to be true. This is one of those areas where perception is far more important than reality, and this young pilot perceives his employer as being willing and able to keep crooked books successfully. He learned that attitude from someone, and I'd guess he learned it from other employees. I'd further guess that this belief is widespread.

The airline industry has big problems, and future labor negotiations are critical; in some cases they could be the difference between survival and bankruptcy.

Is it possible that negotiators can do a credible job if one side sincerely believes that the other side is lying about the basics and— more importantly—getting away with it? This thought terrifies me. The question is not so much, "Is it true?" as it is, "How can we negotiate when some believe it to be true?"

Remember when you heard the same thoughts about Pan Am, Eastern, and Braniff? Remember what happened?

We must also wonder how this came to be. What have carriers done to cause such disbelief? Some management is quick to say it is impossible to get along with unions, but never forget that Southwest does get along with unions and makes steady profits doing it. Is it because management shoots straight with employees? Maybe all airline managers should study under Herb Kelleher.

Southwest also has a wonderful video pointing out that airlines can and do go bankrupt. Maybe all airline labor negotiations should begin with a showing of that video.

Ralph's Update:

I still get upset about this. That young fellow was sharp, had done all the right things, and worked so hard.

☆☆☆☆

NBAA revisited (Oct 2002)

My first NBAA Convention was in Dallas, about 1984, I believe. Piper had the brand new Cheyenne 400LS for sale. It would do 400 statute miles per hour, and we Piper sales folk were excited about it. We figured Piper would be the big news at NBAA. It didn't happen.

While Piper was busy announcing that they had an aircraft that did go 400 mph, Beechcraft (not Raytheon then, young folks, but Beechcraft) announced that they were going to build an aircraft—the Starship—that would go 400 mph. We Piper types chuckled. After all, we had the real 400-mph airplane at the airport, ready to demonstrate, and ready to sell. Beechcraft had a scale model of the Starship, built by Burt Rutan and company. It flew over the airport. It didn't land. By then we Piper types were scoffing out loud.

Guess who stole the show? Beechcraft, that's who. And they taught us a whole lot about showmanship and the mystique of the fabled Beechcraft name.

That was my first NBAA. With an introduction like that, you'd think I would have a sour taste about NBAA's big show, but I don't. I love the thing, if only because it is just so, well, awesome.

If you ever wonder about the buying power of general aviation, the NBAA show will change your mind. Everybody who is anybody is there, scrambling for their share of the corporate aviation market, and spending a fortune doing it. They come back every year, so you figure they must be getting their money's worth.

If I had to guess, I'd figure the big boys and the would-be big boys—including Cessna, Piper, Boeing, Airbus, Eclipse, Raytheon, Embraer, Bombardier, and a myriad others—must spend well over a million each on their exhibits. The big boys ain't dumb, so you got to figure it's worth it to them.

Cessna claims 424 jet orders announced and/or obtained during the show. No less than 217 of those were the new Mustang, and they tell me those orders all originated during the show. (That's big bucks, and I like to wander around the show and just wonder which of the people I see is capable of buying a jet for a few million.)

On the other end of the scale are small exhibitors with one booth, pushing fabric, nuts and bolts, paint jobs, and other goodies. My city—Huntsville, AL—had a booth, manned by our airport's Brooks Kracke, enthusiastically extolling Huntsville as the perfect place to set up industrial plants.

NBAA is so big that many in our industry "piggy back" by having meetings and parties during the show, just to catch the crowd. Women in Aviation International—which has to be one of the fastest-growing groups in our industry—has a successful breakfast.

Ralph's Update:

The Starship lost tons of money—some say it came close to ruining the company—and Raytheon finally bought them all back and disposed of them, as I understand it.

☆☆☆☆

A market shift (Nov/Dec 2002)

As often admitted, my record of predicting aviation's future has included many an embarrassment, such as predictions of the failure of Lear, the Cessna Citation and Caravan, FedEx, and the success of the Burns Aircraft and the Piper Brave. On the other hand, there have been a few successes...

In 16 years (that's my longest job, except with my own company) this column has predicted the growth of charter, air freight, aircraft management (although we did not foresee that so much of that management would be done by fractional ownership companies), the servicing of airlines by FBOs, self-fueling, and recreational flying.

Don't look now, but recreational flying is growing. My first trip to Oshkosh left me wondering if our industry shouldn't be paying more attention to recreational flying. That was at the end of a five-year "aviation downturn" during which *real* aircraft sales sank faster than the Titanic, and it was truly delightful to see a segment of aviation that was upbeat and doing business.

Since then, recreational flying appears to be booming. To see if these appearances were borne out by facts, I checked around. Nobody really has a good, all-inclusive definition of recreational flying, so it is hard to get statistics. Does it include just homebuilts? Does it also include sailplane flying and antique flying? How about homebuilts that go faster than a speeding bullet and must slow down behind a Lear on the ILS into O'Hare? What about warbirds?

One good definition includes all flying for recreation, rather than for transportation. That includes ultralights, Cubs, sailplanes, paragliders, Bearcats, and most homebuilts. Surely some of those can be used for transportation, but most are used to fly just for the fun of it.

Even with that definition, it is hard to measure the growth of recreational flying. Ultralights, for example, need not be registered, so we have no records. We do know, however, that EAA membership has grown by 70 percent during the last 15 years, and that may well be our best indication. Also, the registration of certificated homebuilts is up to 23,000 and growing by about 1,000 aircraft per year. No telling what will happen if the light sport category becomes a reality. (One caveat—this could all come to a screeching halt if TSA/congress decides to outlaw all of this freedom in the name of security.)

There was a time when old-line general aviation folks totally ignored this segment of the business. Many aviation businesspeople said they wanted nothing to do with "lawn furniture that flies." Others felt we should "be nice" to these people because, who knows, someday they might grow up and buy real airplanes. Others wondered at the time if maybe we should look at recreational flying as a new market opportunity, rather than trying to change it.

Today, one can't help but notice little, "mostly-for-fun" airports busily thriving with rec pilots who rent hangar space, buy fuel, and otherwise support those airports. Sailplanes mix with ultralights, antiques, and "real" airplanes, and many people are introduced to aviation by this wildly enthusiastic segment of our industry.

I have a friend who owns and flies a Bonanza for transportation. He is currently hunting a recreational aircraft as a second airplane. Makes you think, doesn't it?

Ralph's Update:

Light sport aircraft and pilots did become fact, and manufacturers rush to compete in that market. Too early to tell how big that market will be, but serious money is being invested, and that's a good sign. My friend, by the way, did indeed buy a two-place aircraft "just for the fun of it," but he sold the Bonanza first. We all worry about the "graying" of our aging general aviation pilots, but I have a feeling many of them will switch to light sport aircraft, just as my friend did.

2003

"Lord of the Rings: The Return of the King" takes best picture. I don't go to fantasy movies,, so didn't see it. Blogs are big and getting bigger. I am inducted into the Alabama Aviation of Fame, thus proving that you really can fool all of the people some of the time. Feds enact a do-not-call list. Concorde crashes in Paris.

Mr. Integrity (Jan/Feb 2003)

Bob Hudgens, the builder of Montgomery Aviation in Alabama, is dead. Many of us will never forget him. Bob Hudgens was one of many who went into aviation at the end of WW II. He was one of the very few who actually made a success of it. He started with nothing but his own work ethic, energy, and abilities, and he made it, big time.

He was a member of the Alabama Aviation Hall of Fame, past president of the National Air Taxi Conference (which became part of the current NATA), a Quiet Birdmen member, past president of the Montgomery Rotary and Chamber of Commerce, and a leader in his church. But he was so much more.

Mr. Hudgens (He was, and always will be, Mr. Hudgens to me.) was ethical to a fault. I met him in 1972 when I worked for National Aviation Underwriters (NAU), and he was my biggest customer. He was a legend at NAU. In the old days, he had refused to buy product liability insurance—can you imagine such a thing in today's world?—and then one of his operations had put jet fuel in a Southern Airlines Martin 404. Nobody was hurt, but it ruined both of those big round piston engines, and that was a chunk of money even back then. Hudgens called his good friend, the president of NAU, and asked, "Do we have any coverage for that?" "No," was the answer, "you don't. We tried to sell it to you and you refused. " That's what I figured," said Mr. Hudgens, and he hung up. Within ten minutes the NAU president called back. "Bob, you're not going to believe this. You do have that coverage! We put it on the policy by mistake, you have been paying the extra premium, and the engines are covered."

Bob's answer created the legend. "Nah," he said, "that's not the deal I made. You just send me a refund of that extra premium." And he hung up again.

I sold to, worked for, and was a friend of the man for more than three decades, and never, ever, saw him fudge on a matter of integrity. When you worked for him, you never had to worry about doing the right thing.

When working for his Piper distributorship, I once sold a Piper Warrior to one of our dealers. As he was writing the check, the dealer asked, "Ralph, do you know if they are ever going to put a high compression engine in the Warrior so it can handle low-lead gas better?" Well, I wasn't supposed to know, but someone at Piper had given me the inside scoop; Piper was indeed putting the high compression engine into the Warrior within the next 30 days. I told the truth, the dealer canceled the order, and Bob Hudgens responded typically, "Well, you did the right thing."

In the late 1970s and early 1980s, prime was 20 percent, our distributorship had millions of dollars in Piper inventory, two more Senecas on order, and nobody was buying. Mr. Hudgens told the Piper rep, in person, that he wanted to cancel the Seneca orders and pay the penalty, as allowed by our contract. Then he added, "But, if Piper would be hurt by that, we will take the Senecas." The rep said, "It will help us if you take them." Mr. Hudgens took them.

Mr. Hudgens ran Montgomery Aviation and all of its derivative businesses for more than half a century. He never missed a payroll.

Quite simply, I loved the man. He had a tremendous influence on my life and helped me long after I went into business for myself.

A lot of what I believe today I learned from him, and he never led me astray. We remained good friends and visited not infrequently during recent years. I saw him the day before he died and shall always be grateful for that last visit.

Ralph's Update:

No update on this one. I like it as is. One of the great things about writing is that you get to write things like this about old friends.

Are we going nuts? (Mar 2003)

Did you think it was funny when that woman sued McDonald's because the coffee burned her? So did I, until she won that not-so-small fortune in court. Did you chuckle when you heard about another woman suing the tobacco company because they never told her that smoking for decades could kill her? I laughed, too, right up until she won big time.

And I never learn. I still thought it was funny when, recently, I found out some nuts are suing McDonald's for making them fat. But I'm not laughing any more.

Now hear this: The February 3 issue of *Fortune* magazine has a cover story entitled, "Is Fat The Next Tobacco?" According to *Fortune*, that goofy "I couldn't stop myself and you-made-me-fat" lawsuit is serious as a heart attack and a forerunner of things to come. To quote: "The war over obesity will be fought in the courts. That's bad news for Big Food."

You should read the article. It speaks of lawyers who fought tobacco but are now shifting eagerly to "fat" lawsuits. It quotes a college prof who speaks of a possible guvmint "implementation plan" to reduce obesity.

At the same time, physicians retire early rather than face the cost and risk of malpractice suits. Airlines threaten to quit hauling pets rather than deal with increased guvmint regulation. We are bringing fewer new drugs to the marketplace as the cost of jumping through guvmint hoops to gain approval climbs ever higher.

Will the time eventually come when nobody produces anything because it is just too risky? How can we compete worldwide—which we surely must do to survive—if we must support ever-increasing layers of guvmint regulation to make sure that everybody is protected from everything? Is there to be no individual responsibility left in our country?

Ah, you say, thank goodness I am not in the food business. This madness won't affect me. Hogwash!

When the costs of goods and services go up, it changes everything for everybody. That matters more now than ever before, because we compete worldwide rather than just in our back yard.

Much of aviation's income is derived from business-to-business sales. We cannot survive if the rest of business is in the dumps.

Besides, remember the fellow who ran a Cub into a truck a few years back, then sued because Piper designed a faulty airplane back in the 1930s? Have we forgotten all of those product liability suits? We're in this right now and have been for decades. It's just getting worse. There is no aircraft that won't bite if the pilot ignores the laws of physics. Does that mean every crash will produce huge court losses?

Business produces goods/services when the estimated cost of doing so is less than the estimated income to be thus derived. Any time—repeat, any time—that is not true, business backs off. When business backs off, all hell breaks loose.

Business takes huge risks in this country, and that risk is borne by investors seeking profit. Increase costs and the likelihood of profits drops. Then investment drops. Will it eventually stop? How long will we continue to reward irresponsibility?

These things worry me.

Ralph's Update:

It's not just the lawsuits—it's all the rules, too. Did you ever notice all that black plastic sheeting draped around construction sites to curtail erosion? I wonder how the heck we're going to compete worldwide when our competitors don't have to use it. How long can we keep paying taxes to fund all of our silly rules when we are so desperately engaged in such fierce competition? Didja ever get the idea that we just don't get it?

⇨⇨⇨⇨

Time to stand out (Apr 2003)

Travel may be more hassle than ever, but even worse is the hassle of buying stuff. Used to be, the seller had to be nice to the buyer, and that's still true when I am the seller. When I am the buyer, somebody has somehow changed the rules.

Everyone I buy from has a telephone answering system that is designed to let me, the buyer, know that my time is worth zilch, nada, zip, zero, while the seller's time is as valuable as a bomb shelter in Baghdad. The answering system first informs me that I can save time and money by contacting the seller's website. That is a pernicious lie. The website is incomprehensible. God couldn't buy anything on that website without prior training in hell.

Just today—true story—I called a company to buy its product. The answering machine let me know that if I didn't want to be overcharged and abused, I should go to the seller's website. I did. It didn't work. In desperation, I recalled the phone number, and they connected me with someone who could "walk" me through the web site, strongly implying that this lady was on the payroll to deal with the mentally impaired. She talked clearly, distinctly, calmly, and slowly, so as not to exceed my mental capabilities or agitate me. I explained to the old bat that I am a Rhodes Scholar, a Nobel Prize winner, and a NASA rocket scientist, but to no avail. I got the full treatment.

This woman's first job is to make the buyer feel like an incompetent fool. She asks questions until she can find some way to say, "Oh, well, of course it won't work if you do it that way!" Then, having put me in my proper place, she really did try to help. The exercise ended 15 minutes later when she finally asked what I wanted to buy. "Oh," she said, "you can't buy that online!"

Y'all, I laughed out loud. She was silent for a second, then she laughed just as loudly. (The seller, by the way, is a large and well-known company. It is also currently operating in bankruptcy, and I couldn't stop myself from telling her that I could understand how they got there. Then we both had a good laugh.)

There is one bit of wonderful news in all of this. In today's world, if you can figure out any way to provide old-fashioned sales and services, you will appear to be a business genius right up there with Walton, Welch, and Gates. Never since man swapped the bow and arrow for tools of production has it been so easy to shine in the marketplace.

This is one area where the local business/airport has the edge. You can still serve the customer personally, and there is nothing the customer wants more. I've said it before and it is still true: The charter customer is much more impressed by an attentive crew and a sandwich tray than by pressure differential and shaft horsepower. Good service is more valued than a few cents per gallon. People still like to be treated the way customers used to be treated.

Surely the airport that reduces the post-September 11 hassle factor will look like Eden before the snake got in.

Ralph's Update:

The only thing that has changed is that the people who answer are now apt to be located "offshore." Some of them I can understand, some I can't. I talk with those I can understand, and tell the others, "I'm sorry, but I can't understand you. I'm going to hang up and call back. Maybe I will luck up and reach someone I can understand." Some folks say that's mean and crude, but why should we pretend?

Service master (May 2003)

Computers, like airlines, have come to be considered almost a commodity. Americans buy computers and airline tickets the same way we buy milk, gasoline, and shaving cream: "Just give me the cheapest, because I can't tell the difference in quality between any of them."

I just bought a new laptop to replace my old and hated Gateway, and I bought the new one from the one firm I know that will service it.

This time I rebelled. I bought the new laptop from North Alabama Computer Associates (NACA), the folks who have repaired our computers for the last few years. A fellow named Terry runs their service department, and oh, it is such a joy to have someone I can actually reach on the telephone or even drop by to see. Some days the entire computer industry decides—just for the fun of it—to mess up everything I touch, computerwise. (Wife Gail says that's silly, that "they" don't do that. I know better. There is a club of them. Bill Gates is president, and they get together at least once a week and say, "Hey, let's sock it to that fat guy in Alabama. You know, what's his name?" On those days, I go cussing and screaming to Terry. He calms me and fixes the computer. He deserves the Nobel Prize.)

I did not compare prices or brands on the new laptop. I did not read ads, ask friends, or shop around. I went to NACA only, and they wouldn't even haggle over price. I bought a computer that they put together themselves. I have no idea how it compares to other brands. I do know that I could have purchased the same features cheaper. But I didn't want features; I wanted Terry.

I took my new laptop home, and, of course—duh!—I couldn't make it work right. I took it straight back to Terry and he fixed it in five minutes. That's exactly why I bought from NACA, and I am as happy with my new laptop as a hog in a barrel of Arkansas garbage after a weekend barbecue cookoff.

The customer will pay extra for desired benefits, when the customer knows that you offer those benefits. Here's a crying shame: I knew about NACA long before I bought my detested Gateway laptop. They built a desktop for wife Gail years before that, and I knew about Terry's service. But I did not know that NACA could make laptops, too. Terry told me that, himself, one of the many times he fixed the accursed Gateway. I had long since given up on getting any service from Gateway, and I decided that very day that my next laptop would come from NACA. They had that sale locked up for years before I even met their salesperson.

How about your business? Is your service department building up future sales or irritating customers who have already bought? Do service customers know what other products you sell? Remember, your "service" department includes any person who serves the customer, be that a CFI, charter pilot, front-desk person, or airport security person.

When I sold airplanes for a living, most of my sales came from the service department, charter department, and flight school department. It does work.

Ralph's Update:

Lord, I hated that Gateway. Two and a half years later, I still have the replacement laptop purchased from NACA. Son Kevin, who travels much of the world—India, Germany, Israel, and England, so far—helping computer users solve problems, says that's a pretty long time for a laptop that travels. He strongly implies that it is a miracle for someone so easily befuddled and rankled by computers as I.

Turn of a page (Jun 2003)

The Concorde retires this year, and some call it the end of an era. If so, it is an era in which we Americans did not participate. Way back in 1963, John Kennedy brought up the idea of a supersonic transport aircraft. It was the wave of the future, and of course America should lead the way.

In 1969, Nixon approved the American SST, which existed on paper as the Boeing 2707-2000. Most of us thought it was about time. The Russkies had already beaten us to it—their TU-144 SST first flew in 1968. Déjà vu; it was Sputnik all over again. (You young folk will never fully understand the agonizing horror that Sputnik represented to America. It turned our world upside down; we were no longer master of all things. Could it be possible that God was not on our side after all? Now, with the SST, we had done it again. The Russians had it and we did not.) The English and French were close behind with the Concorde.

To my utter disgust and amazement, Congress actually killed the American SST in 1971. The country of the Wright Brothers, Lindbergh, Doolittle, and the moon shot had abdicated the throne! What was the world coming to? I hung my head in shame and complained mightily. "Oh," lamented I, "we will be so sorry in a few short years when all the world travels supersonically on aircraft made by Russia, England, and France." Well, I was wrong.

In the first place, Congress didn't really kill the airplane, but just killed any guvmint subsidy thereof. That was before I became leery of any project not funded by greedy investors on the free market. I have since learned that lesson well and have become suspicious of businesspeople who want the guvmint to pay up-front costs (or bail out the airlines).

As it turned out, the SST had problems from day one. The Russians crashed the TU-144 at the 1973 Paris Air Show, ceased production not long thereafter, and retired the airplane in 1983. In what became known as the Battle of New York, The Big Apple forbade any SST until 1977, when—begrudgingly—they finally allowed Concorde operations.

What was worse, it soon became apparent that despite enormous guvmint subsidies the Concorde would never—could never—break even, much less turn a profit. That, of course, was the beginning of the end. The much-publicized Concorde crash outside of Paris was another deep blow, despite the Concorde's otherwise good record over the years.

Still, it was mostly the sin of unprofitability that brought down the Concorde, and rightly so. Faced with increasing maintenance costs for the aging aircraft, France and England have finally cried uncle, and who can blame them?

Richard Branson, of Virgin Atlantic fame, tried to buy the Concorde, but the Brits said, "Jolly bad show," and the French cried, "Non, non," as the French are wont to do. Methinks they feared the brash fellow might have made it profitable, and they couldn't have that, now, could they. (Me also thinks Branson was lucky they turned him down, but who knows?)

Ralph's Update:

Now, the SST is in the news again, four decades after the idea first reared its head. The new one—if it really comes true—will be a general aviation airplane funded by investors. That's unbelievable and exciting. As usual, I hope it happens. We'll see.

Fractional math (Aug 2003)

Once upon a time, long ago and far away, a gloom descended across the land. Money ceased to flow into Wichita, aircraft ceased to emerge from factories, and the people were sore afraid. Then a great voice said, "Let there be fractionals!"

Lo, the sun arose, the gloom evaporated, and once again happiness reigned in the land of general aviation.

Folks, it was danged near that dramatic.

It would be truly difficult to overestimate the impact of fractionals on general aviation. All of a sudden, all God's chillun got a piece of an airplane, and a new, turbine airplane at that. Rivets are bucked, engines are built, avionics are installed, charter thrives, pilots fly, and fuel flows, all because of fractionals.

And I wonder, as the country song goes, "Why didn't I think of that?"

Today, even as everybody in the country rushes to expand the fractional idea to include owner-flown piston aircraft, the original big boys of fractionals are perhaps moving into phase two.

An early indication of this came a few years ago when NetJets gave a presentation at Exxon's Tiger Spirit dealer meeting. The speaker pointed out that it had indeed been proved that profit could be made *selling* fractionals; now they had to prove they could make a profit *operating* those aircraft. I do not recall that a tremor went through the industry at that time, but it might well have been appropriate.

Fractionals have become major buyers of jet fuel and thus very important to traditional FBOs. Furthermore, fractional operators stated from day one that they intended to stay in their core business, and harbored no desire to expand into the FBO end of the industry. Now, we have to wonder if that is changing.

Large fractional operators have already been haggling for fuel, and why should anyone be surprised? Large fuel customers have always haggled, and fractional operators certainly qualify as large customers. The question now is how far will this go? So far, they seem to be happy haggling for fuel contracts with and through the FBO, but how long will that last?

Seeking lower costs and/or better service, will they eventually choose to become FBOs themselves? Remember, we saw this happen in the early days of corporate aviation. At any airport where a fractional operator is a major customer of fuel and services, sooner or later the idea of becoming the provider will almost assuredly arise. If history repeats, this idea will loom largest where service is poor and/or prices rapacious.

Good service and reasonable prices—delivered by friendly, enthusiastic people—have always been important when it comes to hauling important people in expensive aircraft. Pilots and aircraft operators are at least as concerned with the care of their passengers as they are with price. The fixed base operator who provides great service is much less likely to lose a big customer over a few cents per gallon.

Ralph's Update:

No update here—the jury is still out on this one.

2004

"Million Dollar Baby" takes best picture. Bush wins again in spite of much argument about Iraq War. Great discussion of blue and red states. The Red Sox end the curse of the Bambino. Ronald Reagan dies. Flu vaccine shortage.

Jobs and elections (Mar 2004)

Election years are tough on me. Truth is, I don't believe that guvmint has answers; the free market has answers. From now 'til November, politicians will scare me to death explaining what they would do for my benefit. The main thing I want them to do is leave the free market alone.

So far, it seems that each pol is out to convince the public that he (or she) hates and fears the free market more than any other pol. I am appalled. (This is a bipartisan activity; I still haven't forgiven "W" for the steel tariffs.) Now hear this: All voters should be required to read the article, "Peter Drucker Sets Us Straight," in the January 12, 2004, issue of *Fortune* magazine.

No matter who does the measuring, Peter Drucker would be on any Top 10 list of influential business consultants/writers. The article explains who Drucker is and why he's important. I'll just point out that the man gave us the phrases "privatization" and "management by objective," among many other things.

Drucker is 94 years old now, and I approached this article wondering what the old man had left to say. I had forgotten that only a few years ago he was called—in a *Forbes* magazine article—"still the youngest mind" in the country. The current *Fortune* article left me stunned, as has everything else I have read by or about the man.

The pols rant and rave about us exporting jobs. Says Drucker, "Nobody seems to realize that we import twice or three times as many jobs as we export."

That statement knocked me for a loop. Drucker's logic is simple and irrefutable. If we export jobs when we open a factory in Asia, then just as certainly we are importing jobs when Japan and Germany open factories in Alabama. Damn! That hit me like a thunderbolt.

Drucker goes on to explain that we are actually "…exporting low-skill, low-paying jobs but are importing high-skill, high-paying jobs." He points out that the U.S. industries "that are moving jobs out of the U.S. are the more backward industries," and that "…the U.S. remains the cheapest place in the world to produce for many of the more advanced industries."

Worried about unemployment? Drucker points out that we "have the highest proportion of our population in the workplace by far than any other country in the industrial world." He explains that we have the greatest opportunity for educated workers, with "basically no unemployment for college graduates."

Find out why Drucker believes the way we measure productivity is out of date, and why productivity is probably higher than we think. Find out also the one thing that does worry him about our economy.

Then, please, tell other people about this article. The pols tell the public that we are in serious trouble and only they can save us. It just ain't so. We the people are doing quite well. It's guvmint that needs to be straightened out.

Ralph's Update:

Drucker lived 'til late 2005 and was quoted and cited by some of our best business publications right up to the end. He was a truly brilliant man and will be sorely missed.

A sign of change (Sept 2004)

In 1970 (was it really that long ago?) a popular song complained about "Signs, signs, everywhere signs." Evidently, signs made the singers mad; but I like signs everywhere, particularly at airports. It should be possible—even easy—to drive into any city and follow signs to the airport, then to arriving and departing flights, parking options, and general aviation.

Inside the terminal there should be signs directing the innocent visitor from any location to gates, restaurants, ground transportation, baggage claim, ticket counters, and restrooms. Particularly restrooms.

Although airports come closer to this ideal than other places in most cities, there is room for improvement. (At one airport recently, I arrived at a sign advising me to turn both left and right for my gate. A nearby skycap said the sign "been like that a long time. I keep tellin' 'em, but they don't do nothin'.")

I asked Paula Hochstetler, head of the Airport Consultants Counsel (ACC), for the name of an expert on airport signage, and she sent me to Joe Erhart, Apple Designs, Inc. (ADI). Joe literally wrote the FAA-recommended book on the subject—"Guidelines for Airport Signing and Graphics"—and he knew more answers than I had questions.

First, Joe taught me that correct terminology is not signage, but rather "information systems." That covers all of the information needed for wayfinding, flight schedules, notices, and other info needed by those who use airports. He also pointed out that a good system would have both printed and voice directions in multiple languages. I hadn't even thought of that.

One gripe I have is that signage in most airport check-in areas is totally inadequate. Should you go to counter or kiosk? Take your bags to TSA or airline counter? In what order should you do all this? Marco Polo couldn't decipher the mystery—how can little old ladies who travel twice per year cope?

Erhart explained that TSA put out rules in early 2002. A national taskforce of the ACC, with Joe as chair, carefully opined to TSA that the rules missed the boat in some ways. TSA was receptive, but, before progress could be made, the whole problem was turned over to the Department of Homeland Security (DHS), which plans to come up with new rules.

In the meantime, no airport wants to spend money on new information systems knowing that new DHS rules might change everything. In other words, progress is waiting on the same guvmint that was—via TSA—going to standardize security at airports across the country.

So what else is new? Well, as I write this, DHS has contacted Joe's taskforce, asking for examples of airports that do a good job on info systems. DHS will study those airports before writing the new rules. Finally, the taskforce will be asked to review and critique the new rules before they are applied.

We are getting somewhere.

Ralph's Update:

This is still a problem. Particularly irritating to me are those airports that—by design—won't use signs that project outward from a counter, restroom, or gate. A pox on them. The purpose of signs is to direct. That purpose should take precedence over some imagined need for artistic design. At one airport recently there was no sign directing me to rental car return until I had already passed the terminal. Two poxes on them.

◇◇◇

Local vs. national (Oct 2004)

In his regular column—Inside the Fence—in September, editor John Infanger addresses two of the biggest messes in our world: O'Hare and the Mideast crisis. Nothing timid about Infanger. Danged if I don't believe it would be easier to straighten out the Mideast than the mess that is O'Hare.

What we have at O'Hare is local politics messing up a nationwide system. What the area needs is a new airport. What local politicians (can you spell Daley?) offer is an expansion of O'Hare. Moses could wander for another 40 years—possibly in a holding pattern at O'Hare—before finding peace in this political imbroglio. Maybe we would all be better off if Da Mayor bulldozed the damned place in the dark of night.

Da Mayor says O'Hare can be expanded/improved to be much more efficient. No doubt that is true. But it will still be a nightmare to get to, the parking lots will no doubt be even farther from the gates, and I, for one will still avoid the place like the plague.

The city needs another airport, but that ain't possible without diluting (rather than strengthening) the power of Da Mayor. One airport—in Gary, IN—already exists and even has plans to bootstrap growth with dollars derived from the growth itself. (What a novel idea.)

Right now, the FAA has asked the airlines to limit or adjust their arrivals/departures at O'Hare to cut congestion. That's like asking Sax Fifth Avenue to cut its sales to solve the congestion in New Yawk City.

Atlanta and Philadelphia have the same problems and may likewise be asked to limit service. Can we spot a trend here? Philadelphia, they tell me, is the largest city in America with only one airport served by airlines. Atlanta is the second largest. I don't know from diddley about Philadelphia, but Atlanta plans expansion of Hartsfield-Jackson Airport rather than building a second airport.

(It used to be just Hartsfield Airport, named after a former mayor. They added Jackson, the name of another former mayor, but the expanded name did nothing to improve the congestion.)

Once again, local politics seem to be the main reason. A second Atlanta airport has been suggested in several different spots, but the not-in-my-backyard philosophy is alive and well in Georgia. My brother lives in Gwinnett County, one of the suggested locations, and he points out that more people live in Gwinnett County than in Atlanta—and "We will never let Atlanta put their airport or their rapid transit system in our county."

The market does help. Many of my traveling friends already avoid O'Hare, Philly, and Atlanta when possible, just as I do. "But Ralph," people tell me, "that's not fair. Those cities do a good job considering the traffic they handle." Hey, I don't care less why those airports are miserable places to change airplanes; I just know that they are, and that I avoid misery whenever possible.

Ralph's Update:

Is there really a solution for those three cities? Maybe not. NASA rocket engineers tell me that there's a limit to how much water you can shove through a pipe of a given diameter. Just as surely, there's a limit to how many people can be shoved through these three airports.

Sound of money (Nov/Dec 2004)

Show me the money! That expression sums up the cynicism of our society. Show me the money, or I won't believe you. If you want to believe in the future of aviation, I hope you were at NBAA's annual convention and trade show in Vegas, 'cause that's where the money was.

The full stats are elsewhere in this issue, but I will tell you that the trade show had a record number of exhibiting companies. A record number of companies bellied up to the bar and laid their money down to exhibit. That doesn't guarantee our future, but it does show that some mighty successful businesspeople do believe that we have a future, and a good one at that.

Companies like Boeing, Airbus, Gulfstream, and Bombardier were there, and their exhibits alone cost more than any airplane I know how to crank. They were staffed by corporate types with blue suits, silk ties, and shoes that gleamed with a gentle luster to which my Rockports cannot even aspire.

And there was something new this year. The big buzz was the announcements of two—not one, but two—supersonic bizjets by two companies, Aerion and SAI. Both include big names in aviation, finance, and design, and both sound like they know what they're doing.

The numbers alone make your head swim. We're talking 4,000 miles range at Mach 1.6 to 1.8. We're also talking about laying out billions, repeat billions, of dollars over the next eight years or so before the aircraft will be ready to sell at a retail price in the neighborhood of $80 million—give or take a few million.

I am struck dumb with wonderment. How can anybody plan ahead that far, raise the money, pay the bills, hold it all together, and make a profit eight years down the road? The people with the money think they can do it, and they're willing to invest that money to prove it. More power to them and I hope they succeed.

Along those same lines, I went to a much smaller aviation meeting recently. Burt Rutan, builder of SpaceShipOne and Voyager, and one of the hottest people in aviation, was in Huntsville, AL, meeting with NASA folks. Burt agreed to speak for free in a hangar at my favorite grass strip, Moontown Airport. Details were handled by EAA Chapter 190, FBO/airport manager George Myers, and a zillion volunteers. For no charge we got supper and a Burt Rutan speech with plenty of time for autographs and photo ops. (Many gawkers stood in line shamelessly to get their pictures taken with Rutan. You can see my picture at www.ralphhood.com.)

Rutan pointed out that aviation grew rapidly after the Wright Brothers' first flight as entrepreneurial types competed to build airplanes. Many of those airplanes were failures, but we learned from the failures. Rutan believes we are about to see a burst of growth in space, now that SpaceShipOne has proved that private money and efforts can reach it. In fact, Rutan already has an order from Sir Richard Branson, Virgin Atlantic airlines, for five larger spaceships. Sir Richard has the money (this is the guy who tried to buy the Concordes when they quit flying) and believes he can make a profit flying tourists into space.

Ralph's Update:

We can't update this one for years. Will there be a corporate SST? Will the Branson/Rutan team really make money flying pax into space? Who knows?, but ain't it exciting!

2005

Michael Jackson's trial is big news story of the year. Southern states participate in Hurricane-of-the-Week Program. Camilla and Prince Charles marry, visit USA.

A380 connection (Apr 2005)

I feel so important (but first, a little background music). Airbus gets a lot of media play these days with the A380, the aircraft that makes the 747 look like an ultralight. I particularly enjoy the television coverage just because it strongly features John Leahy, Airbus chief commercial officer. That gives me the chance to mention—casually—to everyone in the room, "I know John. Known him for years."

It's true. Leahy taught classes for us Piper sales types in the 1970s and early 1980s, and even engaged me as a speaker once. It is not exactly true that John calls me for advice these days, although I imply that he does.

Leahy was a good teacher. He bobbed and weaved like a prizefighter as he explained the intricacies of aircraft finance, seven-year cash flow projections, spread sheets, and net present value cost—right sophisticated stuff. In college he had toiled as a flight instructor and flown night freight in Aztecs, so he also knew the gritty side of the business. We learned a lot from Leahy.

When Leahy left Piper, times were tough in aviation, and I called to ask about his plans. I remember his answer well. He said that a lot was happening in aviation in Europe and he was going to check it out. I remember thinking the boy was going to do well, but I never dreamed he would one day be a major player for an international company. Shows what I knew. (I made the same mistake about Pete Correll, one of my high school classmates. I figured Pete would do pretty well; he ended up chairman and CEO of Georgia-Pacific. Makes more money in a year than I will make in my lifetime.)

I wanted to write about the A380, and I got to wondering if I could get Leahy on the phone now that he is—in all honesty and with no tongue in cheek—an international business big shot. I decided to try.

That week I was speaking at Aviation Industry Week in Vegas and to Women in Aviation in Dallas. Leahy was jet-setting back and forth between California and France. He was on the ground when I was in the air and vice versa; the split in time zones didn't help. After four days of international telephone tag, Mary Anne Greczyn of Airbus's PR department actually got us together on the phone.

I asked John if the things he taught us in the 1970s were useful for selling jumbo jets internationally. "Ralph," he said, "you'll be proud to know that we use every bit of that. The big difference is that airliners are income producers and must make a profit." He still sells features and benefits, but the bottom line provides the biggest benefit. (I remembered that from selling crop dusters in Mississippi, but that doesn't sound half as sophisticated.)

Interesting. What John taught us more than two decades ago he uses today to sell the ultimate big-ticket item. Tell the truth, that class also helped me with everything I've sold since.

Lesson learned.

Ralph's Update:

One of the nice things about aviation is that the industry is new enough and small enough that if you hang around long enough you'll meet some of the industry greats. Some of us are just uncool enough to get a big kick out of that!

Focus on service (May 2005)

"The era of cheap oil is over," said Venezuelan president Hugo Chavez in March. Everyone else seems to agree. Those waiting for oil prices to drop probably ain't gonna live that long. Alternative fuels will eventually abound but will not be as cheap in the foreseeable future as oil was in the memorable past. Get used to it.

Airlines cut costs where possible, including cutting customer services. Today's paper announced the closing of several more executive clubs, and most such clubs that remain open ain't what they used to be. (I finally quit using the things when they began to resemble the Blue Light Special at Kmart.)

And airlines renegotiate with airports (a la Northwest vs. Minneapolis area airports). To the extent their negotiations are successful, airports must then cut costs themselves and look for other revenue sources. Maybe the general aviation side of the airport? Airport vendors?

The inevitable result is a tightening up in all facets of aviation. It would be very easy to end up with a snarling, nasty airport environment, wherein everybody is meaner than Bad, Bad Leroy Brown, who was, according to Jim Croce's song, "meaner than a junkyard dog." That includes the customer who takes the brunt of all the above.

The big job will be maintaining friendly customer service under pressure. We can all learn from watching the failures and successes of the airlines.

We passengers felt the difference instantly when the airlines finally decided that the customer really did want low fares and was seemingly unwilling to pay more for better service. I am honestly convinced that some airlines told employees that, "if passengers want cheap fares they're going to have to suffer."

What the legacy carriers didn't seem to understand was that discount airlines provide the friendliest service in the industry. Yes, you might have to wait in longer lines, live on peanuts, and fight for the good seats; but in the meantime, the flight attendants smile, flirt, and recite funny poetry.

As prices climb and amenities decrease, it is hard to remember that friendly service—service with a smile—becomes more important than ever. That smile costs little and means a lot. It's one of the few benefits you can offer that cost nothing.

Management must be very good at motivating employees to take pride in friendly service under tough conditions. If the boss talks about cheap customers, that attitude will be—not might be, but will be—passed along to customers by frontline employees. It is management's job to sell the truth. ("Customers are our bread and butter and we need to keep them happy. Especially now that it is so important.")

Service with a smile. It costs nothing, matters a lot, and is difficult to achieve because it requires leadership.

Ralph's Update:

Funny thing about customer service. I have been teaching it for lo, these many years and in every class there is always somebody who will sidle up during the coffee break to tell me, "Customer service won't solve everything." Hell, everybody knows that, but customer service will help solve everything.

□□□□

Power economics (Jun 2005)

It's started. On May 2 it was announced that Neiva, a subsidiary of Embraer, has delivered the first certificated production aircraft powered by ethanol—a crop duster. The company next plans to convert passenger aircraft to operate on ethanol.

Funny thing about this. For years, folks have been urging our guvmint to push subsidies and force the use of ethanol over oil-based fuels. For years, I have argued that ethanol will be used when ethanol delivers more energy per dollar than gasoline. In Brazil—which is short on oil, long on the ability to grow sugar cane—that is true today. Arguably, that is also now true in the U. S. of A. If it isn't, it most likely soon will be.

The advantages of ethanol are largely two-fold: It's cleaner and it's renewable. Thus we can do good for the environment and kick our dependence on outside oil all in one fell swoop. According to ethanol boosters (most loudly represented by agricultural interests), this is ample reason for the guvmint to get involved. On the other hand, Americans are not interested unless ethanol is cheaper.

Many say it should be forced upon us by increasing the taxes on oil-based fuels or providing subsidizes on ethanol. Indeed, we currently have a half-dollar-per-gallon tax credit on ethanol. The other side (loudly represented by oil interests) says ethanol is too expensive, particularly when you consider the infrastructure changes required.

We already have refineries that produce gasoline, trucks that deliver it, service stations that pump it, and engines that burn it. A massive shift to ethanol for cars, airplanes, lawn mowers, and trucks would require some combination of duplicating and/or replacing all of that infrastructure.

On the other hand, if there's one thing we can do in this country, it's produce grain and deliver it (cheaply) to the market. We can flat do that job, perhaps better than any other country in the world. It makes you wonder why we are so terrified of expensive oil. We might even profit from a switch to ethanol. After all, we already export grain. (If we in the South ever figure out how to convert kudzu into fuel, the South really might rise again.)

Ethanol, of course, is not the only alternative fuel being touted as oil prices climb. Diesel, fuel oil, nuclear power, hydrogen, and wind power are being pushed by big boys and girls who are putting their money where their mouths are. One company has invested in converting coal into fuel oil. The Germans did that in WW II, then quit in the face of cheap oil. Now, perhaps, the process will make a profit. In the meantime, Diamond's twin-engine diesel aircraft is selling all over.

It is happening. It is an exciting time to be alive and watching.

So, which alternative fuel will end up on top? What should the guvmint do about all of this? Sit back and watch, that's what. Let the market sort it all out. Anybody want to take bets on that happening?

Ralph's Update:

It really is an exciting time to be alive and watching aviation! Everything is changing, and nobody knows where it will all end. Corporate SSTs, diesel engines, liquid cooling, parachutes on airplanes, airports adjusting to an evergrowing world, private spaceships—it's more fun than a game of spin the bottle was in the seventh grade.

Imminent threat (Aug 2005)

Eminent domain was first explained to me when I was in the second or third grade by my father, who was a school superintendent. He said it lets the guvmint buy property from a few people when all the people need the property for a school. It was an incomplete explanation, but a good one. Now that's all changed.

Our Supreme Court, in its infinite wisdom, has decided that the guvmint can force a lot of people to sell their property when a few people want it to make a profit. It is one of the few times I have seen the Supreme Court act in a way that was/is clearly wrong—as in immoral.

What does this have to do with airports? Think about it. Every private airport I know would make a great shopping center or real estate development. Airports are typically large parcels with but one owner, flat, have good drainage, out in the open, near population centers, and pay less property tax than a good shopping center would. And airports have one other characteristic that makes them particularly vulnerable: They have few friends and many enemies. Neighbors would love to see the property changed to something "useful" like a shopping center.

Will North Alabama's Moontown and Hazel Green airports quickly become developments with houses which are, as the song says, "all built out of ticky-tacky and they all look just the same"? In the case of Moontown, who will lament the fact that hundreds flew their first solo there? That the EAA Chapter meets there and that a fly-in breakfast is held there monthly? Will the local guvmint care that the airport has been written up in *AOPA Pilot*? Or that Burt Rutan spoke there recently?

For that matter, what if local guvmints ever notice that small publicly owned airports could be converted to developments that pay more taxes?

****

Change of subject: Many people try to predict the future. I have a hard enough time just trying to figure out what's happening right now. Most trends are over before I even realize what they are or that I am participating. Every now and then, however, I find a book that explains current events so well that even I can understand. I am currently reading—am engrossed in—just such a book.

"The World Is Flat," by Thomas Friedman—a great book with an improbable title—maintains that the computer has flattened the barriers to worldwide trade, thus making the world flat. What we're talking about here is globalization, and this book explains the basics brilliantly. I won't give you a book review, but will say that the three most important points, as I read it are that (1) globalization is nothing more than doing business with each other; (2) it's a good thing; and, (3) nobody can stop it. Your/our only options are to take part or die on the vine.

Those that think this book doesn't apply to them and their job/business are already behind the eight ball. Buy a copy of "The World Is Flat," read it, and keep it as a reference text.

Ralph's Update:

This update was fun to write. The American public rose up in fury against this use of imminent domain. My state, Alabama, was one of several to pass a local law prohibiting such chicanery and thank goodness. The book, "The World Is Flat" turned out even bigger than expected. Maybe—finally—the world will figure out that trade restrictions are bad things and we will dwell in the house of the free market forever.

A touch of class (Sept 2005)

Wash Pringle is dead. Chances are you never met Wash, but if you did, you never forgot him. When I went to work with Montgomery (AL) Aviation in the 1970's, Wash was there, and he was one of the best linemen who ever parked an airline.

Wash was a world-class tip hustler in the best sense of the word. He didn't hunt for tips so much as he hunted for ways to earn tips. He got the nickname 'Wash' by washing cars for free. Whenever a based customer parked his car, Wash was right there, with his helpful demeanor and delightful voice, saying something like, "Dr. Smith, if you gonna be gone a day or two jes leave me your keys and I'll clean your car for you." Quite often Dr. Smith did exactly that, and you can bet Wash was right there, car keys in hand, to welcome Dr. Smith back home. The car wash was free; the tip tended to the generous side.

Wash once said of the younger linemen, "They call themselves workin' the line. Most of the time they sittin' in the line shack, readin' that "Playboy" magazine when we aren't busy. I'd rather be makin' some money." And he did.

Some FBOs might have forbidden Wash to clean cars on company time, but our "big" boss, Bob Hudgens, figured Wash made tips by keeping customers happy. Mr. Hudgens considered that a good thing. Wash and Mr. Hudgens had a great respect—even love—for each other (Wash was a pallbearer at Mr. Hudgens' funeral a few years ago and I know that meant a lot to both of them).

It was fun to watch them together. The front desk monitored all frequencies, and when Mr. Hudgens was flying in from a trip they announced code words over the public address system. Wash would be right out front to greet and park the plane, with typical Wash flare. (Wash never walked to park an airplane, he trotted out amidst much gesticulating and dramatic signaling as if that arrival was the most important of the day.)

When Mr. Hudgens climbed out of the airplane, Wash invariably said, "Oh, Mr. Hudgens, I didn' know that was you." Hudgens just as invariably responded, "Bull, Wash, you knew it was me since the front desk warned you on the loudspeaker."

Once our mechanics bet Wash $5 that he couldn't get a tip from the cheapest aircraft owner in town. Shop foreman Earl Smith said, "Ralph, I knew we had lost the bet when Wash started shining the man's shoes as he got into his airplane."

A real grouch flew in one day and addressed Wash with the ultimate racist term. Wash treated the man so well that he tipped him $10—unheard of in those days of real money. When the man returned to depart the next day, Wash had his plane ready and had two cokes in the airplane, iced down in a foam cooler. The man tipped Wash another $10.

Ralph's Update:

We had this column beautifully framed for Wash's widow. It looked so good that Montgomery Aviation's Bill Hudgens, son of Bob Hudgens, had me order another framed copy to hang at Montgomery Aviation. There's nothing more fun than writing something like this about an old friend.

Other books by Ralph Hood:

The Truth & Other Lies
Southern Raised in the Fifties

To order products
or
to inquire about hiring Ralph
to speak for your favorite group,
go to
http://www.ralphhood.com
or call
800-828-3802.